Bilingual Special Education Resource Guide

Bilingual Special Education Resource Guide

Edited by Carol H. Thomas and James L. Thomas

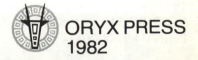

ORYX PRESS
1982

The rare Arabian Oryx is believed to have inspired the myth of the unicorn. This desert antelope became virtually extinct in the early 1960s. At that time several groups of international conservationists arranged to have 9 animals sent to the Phoenix Zoo to be the nucleus of a captive breeding herd. Today the Oryx population is nearing 300 and herds have been returned to reserves in Israel, Jordan, and Oman.

Library of Congress Cataloging in Publication Data
Main entry under title:

Bilingual special education resource guide.

   Bibliography: p.
   Includes index.
   1. Education, Bilingual—United States—Addresses, essays, lectures.   2. Exceptional children
—Education—United States—Addresses, essays,
lectures.   I. Thomas, Carol H.   II. Thomas, James L.,
1945–
LC3719.B54   1982   371.97′0973   82-8149
ISBN 0-89774-008-4   AACR2

Table of Contents

Preface

There are vast numbers of children from diverse cultural backgrounds entering our public schools each year. Many of these children come from families where the dominant language is other than English and, therefore, they often exhibit a limited proficiency in English. In a *New York Times* (20 April 1982) article about the 1980 Census, it was reported that "... one of every 10 people reported speaking a language other than English at home." Rebecca Oxford and others, in "Projections of Non-English Language Background and Limited English Proficient Persons in the United States to the Year 2000" (Rosslyn, VA: InterAmerica Research Associates, Inc., 1980, p. 1), stated that "the non-English language background population is projected to increase from ... 30 million in 1980 to 34.7 million in 1990, and 39.5 million in the year 2000." Additionally, a significant number of bilingual/bicultural children are also considered to be *exceptional* children: children whose mental and/or physical abilities deviate to such an extent that they require special education and/or related services in order to reach their full academic potential.

One of the mandates of PL 94-142, The Education for All Handicapped Children Act, is that *all* handicapped children are to be provided with an "appropriate" education designed to meet their unique needs. When the handicapped child is also a bilingual/bicultural child, the problems involved in identifying needs and in designing and implementing an appropriate education program are multiplied.

While the education of these children appears to be an almost insurmountable task, a number of educators have become actively engaged in the area of bilingual special education and have devoted much of their energies toward developing a better understanding of this special population and its needs. In an attempt to consolidate some of the emerging information about, and the various resources available to serve, the handicapped child who is also racially, culturally, or linguistically different, the editors have compiled this text.

This volume is intended as a resource guide for individuals involved with educational programming for the bilingual special child. The articles in the first part discuss some of the major concerns of bilingual special educators: assessment, curriculum and methodology, social and emotional needs, parent involvement, career education, and teacher education. Information sources in the second part include lists of agencies and centers involved with bilingual special education; teacher training programs; indexes, databases, and journals; and a directory of individuals with expertise in this field who might be contacted to provide lectures, workshops, or consultancy services. The appendix is a list of producers and distributors of bilingual special education materials. A bibliography concludes the volume.

Carol H. Thomas and James L. Thomas

Introduction

BILINGUAL EDUCATION FOR EXCEPTIONAL CHILDREN
FACT SHEET*

What Is Bilingual Education?

Bilingual education refers to school programs for linguistically different children that employ two languages as the media of instruction. One language is English; the other is the dominant or native language spoken in the student's home environment. Some children enter bilingual programs with no knowledge of English, whereas others may have some rudimentary English language skills.

Why Is Bilingual Education Necessary?

Linguistically different children who speak little or no English cannot understand other children or lessons that are presented in English. Not only are these children faced with having to learn new subject matter, they must also learn a new language and often a new culture. It is likely that many of these children will not be able to keep up with the school work and will drop out of school unless there is appropriate intervention. The 1974 Commission on Civil Rights estimated that there were five million linguistically different children in the United States. Evidence exists that 45% of Mexican American children drop out of school before the 12th grade, and the attrition rate for the Native American student is 55%. While the language difference may not be the sole contributor to the academic problems of these children, it is considered by many to be a major factor.

What Are the Goals of Bilingual Education?

Two different philosophies are currently shaping programs in bilingual education: the transitional approach and the maintenance approach.

Transitional Programs. Transitional programs emphasize bilingual education as a means of moving from the culture and language most commonly used for communication in the home to the mainstream of

---

*Reprinted from the ERIC Clearinghouse on Handicapped and Gifted Children, 1979.

American language and culture. Thus, the major goal of a transitional program is to enable the linguistically different child to function in English. The dominant language of the home is used only to help the child make the transition to the English language. In this type of program, the child receives instruction in both languages. The dominant language is gradually phased out as the child becomes more proficient in English.

Maintenance Programs. In contrast to the transitional approach, which has an assimilation orientation, maintenance programs assume a pluralistic approach. The goal of a maintenance program is for the linguistically different child to function in bilingual/bicultural environments. The child's native language and culture are taught concurrently with English and the mainstream culture. The student who completes such a program should be able to function in at least two languages and two cultures.

Garcia (1976) suggested that, while program goals may tend to differ, bilingual programs should focus on three humanistic values: (1) accepting the student's home language; (2) respecting the student's culture and ethnicity; and (3) enhancing the student's self-concept.

Why Is Bicultural Education Often Listed with Bilingual Education?

While most bilingual educators favor maintenance programs, the majority of the programs in existence tend to be transitional. Lack of trained personnel and inadequate funds to support maintenance programs are reasons frequently cited for the predominance of transitional programs. Bilingual educators, however, strongly support the use of bicultural programs, even within the transitional framework. A bicultural emphasis provides the student with a recognition of the value and worth of his/her family's culture and enhances the development or maintenance of a positive self-concept.

What Was the 1974 Lau v. Nichols Supreme Court Decision About?

In 1974, a class action suit on behalf of 1,800 Chinese children was brought before the Supreme Court. The plaintiffs claimed that the San Francisco Board of Education failed to provide programs designed to meet the linguistic needs of these non-English speaking children. This failure, they claimed, was in violation of Title VI of the Civil Rights Act of 1964 and the Equal Protection Clause of the 14th Amendment. They argued that, if the children could not understand the language used for instruction, they were deprived of an education equal to that of other children and were, in essence, doomed to failure.

The school board defended its policy by stating that the children received the same education afforded other children in the district. The position the board assumed was that a child's inability to comprehend English when entering school was not the responsibility of the school, but rather the responsibility of the child and the family. In a unanimous decision, the Supreme Court stated that "under state imposed standards, there was no equality of treatment merely by providing students with the same facilities, textbooks, teachers, and curriculum; for students who do not understand English are effectively foreclosed from any meaningful education." While the court did not mandate bilingual education for non-English speaking or limited-English speaking students, it did stipulate that special language programs were necessary, if schools were to provide equal educational opportunity for such students. School districts with more than 25 minority students must provide a special language program in all academic areas. Hence, the *Lau* decision gave considerable impetus to the development of bilingual education programs.

What Are the Lau Centers?

Nine Lau National Origin Desegregation Assistance Centers were established in 1975, funded through the US Office of Education of the Department of Health, Education, and Welfare under Title IV of the Civil Rights Act of 1964. The centers are located in New York City, Coral Gables, Milwaukee, Denver, Albuquerque, San Antonio, San Diego, Berkeley, and Seattle. These centers serve as helping agencies responsible for providing technical assistance to school districts with enrollments of limited- and non-English speaking children, as well as underachieving linguistically different children.

How Does Legislation Related to Special Education Affect Bilingual Education?

Among the many provisions of Public Law 94-142, the Education for All Handicapped Children Act of 1975, is a provision which mandates a free and appropriate education to all handicapped children. While *appropriate* is not defined as such in the act, the term receives its definition through the Individualized Education Program (IEP) requirement prescribed for each handicapped child. The IEP must address the individual needs of each child, rather than an entire class or category of children. The IEP requires a statement of the specific educational services to be provided in order to meet the student's unique educational needs. Thus, if a handicapped youngster is linguistically different, appropriate programs or services should be written into that student's IEP.

Section 504 of Public Law 93-112, the Rehabilitation Act of 1973, is the basic civil rights provision aimed at terminating discrimination against America's handicapped citizens. The act prohibits exclusion from participation, denial of benefits, or any other form of discrimination against individuals solely by reason of their handicaps. Any program receiving federal financial assistance that is in violation of this regulation may be subject to discontinuation of all federal funds. With a presidential recommendation of 174 million dollars earmarked for bilingual education in fiscal year 1980, it is apparent that handicapped children are entitled to considerable services in the area of bilingual education.

Why Is Bilingual Education of Concern to Special Education?

A number of studies support the contention that there is a disproportionate number of minority students in special education classes. A large number of these students come from linguistically different backgrounds. There is little doubt that there are many special education students who are not receiving an appropriate education because their bilingual educators have not had an adequate background in special education and their special education teachers have had little, if any background, in bilingual education.

What Can Be Done to Improve Services to Linguistically Different Exceptional Children?

There are a number of things that can be done to open the door to better programming for linguistically different exceptional children. Better communication and dialog between the disciplines of special education and bilingual education can start the process. Other specific steps to improve services include:

- More preservice training of all educators in both bilingual and special education.
- More teacher training programs to train teachers, psychologists, and other support personnel in both bilingual and special education.
- Recruitment of special educators who are bilingual to work with linguistically different exceptional learners.
- Inservice programs in the public schools to provide regular education teachers, administration, and support personnel with backgrounds in both special and bilingual education.
- Inservice programs for bilingual educators and for special educators to provide both with insight, understanding, and, in some instances, training in the other's discipline.

Where Can You Get More Information?

National Clearinghouse for Bilingual Education, 1300 Wilson Blvd, Suite B2-11, Rosslyn, VA 22209 (800) 336-4560

REFERENCES

Garcia, R. L. *Learning in Two Languages*. Bloomington, IN: Phi Delta Kappa Educational Foundation, 1976.

Lau v. *Nichols,* 414 U.S. pp. 563–572 (January 21, 1974).

Contributors

Philip C. Chinn is Special Assistant to the Executive Director of Minority Concerns and Development, The Council for Exceptional Children, 1920 Association Drive, Reston, VA. "Curriculum Development for Culturally Different Exceptional Children" is reprinted from *Teacher Education and Special Education* (Summer 1979, vol. 2, no. 4, pp. 49–58). Copyright © 1979 by The Council for Exceptional Children. Reprinted by permission.

George W. Fair is Associate Professor, School of Human Development, University of Texas, Dallas. "Career Opportunities for Culturally Diverse Handicapped Youth" by George W. Fair and Allen R. Sullivan is reprinted from *Exceptional Children* (May 1980, vol. 46, no. 8, pp. 626–31). Copyright © 1980 by The Council for Exceptional Children. Reprinted by permission.

Robert Y. Fuchigami is Professor of Education, Sonoma State University, Rohnert Park, CA. "Teacher Education for Culturally Diverse Exceptional Children" is reprinted from *Exceptional Children* (May 1980, vol. 46, no. 8, pp. 634–41). Copyright © 1980 by The Council for Exceptional Children. Reprinted by permission.

Ronald W. Henderson is Professor of Education and Psychology, University of California, Santa Cruz. "Social and Emotional Needs of Culturally Diverse Children" is reprinted from *Exceptional Children* (May 1980, vol. 46, no. 8, pp. 598–605). Copyright © 1980 by The Council for Exceptional Children. Reprinted by permission.

Robert L. Marion is Associate Professor in the Special Education Department, University of Texas, Austin. "Communicating with Parents of Culturally Diverse Exceptional Children" is reprinted from *Exceptional Children* (May 1980, vol. 46, no. 8, pp. 616–23). Copyright © 1980 by The Council for Exceptional Children. Reprinted by permission.

Nidia Moreno Milne is Assistant Professor in the Department of Educational Psychology, Special Education Program, College of Education, University of Houston—Central Campus, Houston, TX. "Issues and Concerns Related to the Education of Exceptional Bilingual Students" is an ERIC Document in the public domain. Reprinted by permission of the author.

Bilingual Special Education Resource Guide

Part I
Aspects of Dealing with the Bilingual Special Education Student

- Issues and Concerns
- Assessment
- Curriculum Development
- Social and Emotional Needs
- Communication with Parents
- Career Opportunities
- Teacher Education

Issues and Concerns Related to the Education of Exceptional Bilingual Students

by Nidia Moreno Milne

For many years, special educators have expressed concern regarding exceptional bilingual children. This interest has resulted from the multitude of bilingual students and their inappropriate placement in special education settings on the basis of faulty assessment. In fact, simply because "they represent a different culture, possess many different values, and speak a different language than that contained in the schools and standardized tests" (Moreno, 1971), many of these children have been incorrectly diagnosed and labeled as retarded.

Evidence exists in the 1968 finding of the President's Committee on Mental Retardation that children from impoverished and minority group homes were 15 times more likely to be diagnosed as retarded than were children from higher income groups. Jones and Wilderson (1976) note this trend toward racial and special education mainstreaming in their statement:

> Inappropriate tests, poorly trained teachers, or irrelevant curriculum and a failure to understand the intersection of cultural differences and learning problems could be as much to blame for the learning problems as the characteristics and deficits of the children themselves, who typically are labeled ED, LLD, EMR and educated in self-contained classes.

In addition to the rising and broad demand of special educators, such as Moreno, Wilderson, and Jones, for the elimination of activities which degrade and stigmatize children (Reynolds and Birch, 1977), Council for Exceptional Children minority groups have voiced concern for the institutionalized racism and prejudice innate in the excessive placement of minority group children in programs that remove them from the mainstream of education. In response to these concerned outcries, mandates such as

Public Law 94-142 have surfaced. And, fortunately, efforts are now being made to more adequately assess bilingual students in their native languages.

Furthermore, within the current decade, more progressive educational systems have recognized student diversity and have adapted to their individual differences. For example, traditionally, curriculum design and implementation have been based upon the false assumption that all children should learn the same things at the same age and with the same degree of perfection. Although such attempts to force all children into a common mold have proven ineffective, many schools still work within this type of framework, and students who do not conform are penalized or punished. Since no singular grading plan or curriculum can make all students alike, efforts have been made to adjust the curriculum to the children. In addition, minority social and cultural differences have been given increased attention, partly out of concern for their needs and partly in response to their demands (Jaramillo, 1974).

Thus, American society should no longer continue to assume that the middle-class way of life is the only meaningful and valid choice of the many cultures whose life-styles and philosophies radically differ. And, as special educators, we must accept the challenge to achieve within our classes a true reflection of the pluralistic society in which our students live (Jaramillo, 1974). In doing so, we should consider the important issues related to the education of bilingual exceptional children. These issues, discussed below, are: assessment, the monolingual teacher, curriculum and methodology, learning styles, and parent involvement.

ASSESSMENT

In recent years, a great deal of attention has been given to unfair discrimination in student assessment procedures and resultant placement. For example, the famous case of Larry P. in a California law suit (*Larry P. v. Riles,* 1972) resulted in an injunction against the use of IQ tests for minority group children. This case involved findings that showed that several bilingual children had been inappropriately classified as mentally retarded on the basis of intelligence test results. Following this decision, which forced school districts to drop the use of intelligence tests as the sole criterion for placement of children in special education classrooms, there was a sharp reduction in the use of individual IQ tests and in the number of children classified as EMR in California. In a period of about six years following the Larry P. case, enrollments in California EMR classes were virtually halved.

Since most of the intelligence tests used as tools of assessment have been standardized on White middle class students, and/or reflect the linguistic structure of standard English, the placement of a disproportionately large number of Black and Spanish-speaking children into lower educational tracks, such as classes for the educable mentally retarded (Dunn, 1968), can at least partially be attributed to the linguistic and cultural biases of these tests. For example, many Spanish surnamed children have been misplaced in school programs as a result of verbal testing procedures which are biased because they employ a dialect unfamiliar to the bilingual child. That is, the Spanish spoken in the student's home may contain many dialectical variations and Anglicisms.

Non-verbal tests have also been used to ascertain the proposed intelligence of these children. But, these tests are as biased as the verbal ones (Ortega, 1971) because, even after translation, cultural factors may still remain. Mere translation does not eliminate the prejudice, since regional differences within a language make it almost impossible to use a single translation. Yet, a monolingual examiner using a translated test must go strictly by the translated answers which do not allow for regional differences. For example, a Puerto Rican uses the word "toston" to refer to a squashed section of a fried banana. But, to a Chicano, "toston" means "half-dollar." Furthermore, direct translation from one language to another may result in a word or phrase which is not used with the same frequency or which does not have the same potency in the second language. For instance, translating "large egg" into "huevon" may satisfy grammatical requirements and may appear harmless to a translator, but, to Chicanos, it has a more earthy connotation. Monolingual translations are also inappropriate because the language familiar to the non-English speaker is often a combination of two languages, as in the cases of "pocho" and "Tex-Mex" (deAvila, 1975).

In addition to the linguistic factors, these assessments are culturally biased because the home and barrio life of bilingual minority children typically does not provide the tools and experiences tapped by these intelligence tests. So, bilingual students may need practice in test-taking skills.

Therefore, in the past, on the basis of tests, many children have been classified as mentally retarded and have been placed in special education classes, even though these tests are both linguistically and culturally biased (Bryen, 1974).

Special class placement might also be criticized on the grounds of racial discrimination. Mercer (1972) studied the racial and ethnic composition of children in special classes for the mentally retarded in Riverside, California and found three times more Mexican-American and two and one-half times more Blacks in these classes than would be expected by race distribution within the population.

Because relatively high proportions of minority children tend to be classified as exceptional, the claims of assessment bias against minority group children have importance for special education. Thus, the special educator must be aware of this paucity of assessment instruments for use with exceptional bilingual students and must address the need to develop cross-culturally sensitive, criterion-referenced measures in the various academic or skill areas included in the curriculum (deAvila, 1975).

THE MONOLINGUAL TEACHER

Both regular teachers and special educators of bilingual exceptional students need to become aware of the differences of these children—not only linguistically, but also culturally. That is, the monolingual teacher not only may not understand the student's language but also may be ignorant of the values of his/her culture, which may contain features, such as a dislike for personal competition, a present rather than future orientation, and a lack of initiative in problem solving, which conflict with characteristics of the dominant middle-class American culture, making adjustment or acculturation of the bilingual student difficult. Therefore, a need for cultural sensitization of special educators clearly exists.

In the past, there have been efforts to meet this need through inservice programs. But, because personnel—such as curriculum planners, superintendents, and members of boards of trustees—did not appreciate the need for anything other than standard preparation of teachers and standard maintenance of teacher competency, these inservice programs were insufficient. They tended to focus exclusively on teachers, were altogether too short to be effective, and generally gave professionals no opportunity for applied practice in working effectively with minority children. To be effective, these inservice or staff development sessions should address aspects of bilingual education, such as culture, history, law, terminology, rationale, and methodology. In addition, educators should become familiar with the backgrounds and home practices of bilingual/bicultural students and should strive for personal ties and commitments to the ethnic group involved (Bernal, 1972). Bilingual teacher aides can be immensely valuable in alleviating some of these concerns.

CURRICULUM AND METHODOLOGY

The culturally different student brings to the classroom a rich heritage (Jaramillo, 1974), a wealth which may work not only in this particular student's favor but also for the benefit of the entire class. By making use of diverse cultural backgrounds, the special educator can both provide the bilingual exceptional child with a sense of identification and make the class more culturally relevant.

But, because many current teaching strategies, perspectives, and curricula were developed during an era in which it was believed that America was and should be a cultural "melting pot," special education curricula and methodology need to be revised. Technique and materials modification involves creating exciting and interesting instructional tools which stress self-concept, pride in their culture, and academic competence—the three ultimate criteria for any relevant material or curriculum.

When making current materials and methodology appropriate to the bilingual exceptional child,* the special education teacher should consider the following factors:

1. New bilingual education or special education materials.
2. Use of appropriate bilingual, educational television programs.
3. The interfacing and cooperativeness of bilingual education, special education, and the bilingual parent.
4. Training in self-concept and ways of enhancing self-esteem for the bilingual exceptional student.
5. Cultural awareness, cultural values, and language.
6. Research involving bilingual special education.

LEARNING STYLES

Many educators and educational psychologists believe that positive self-concept is necessary for learning (Reyes, 1980). Because positive self-concept is so crucial to learning, teachers of bilingual exceptional children should be aware of the factors influencing this aspect of their students' learning styles.

When a child brings to the classroom a set of cultural patterns which differ from the prevalent White middle-class standards of his/her classmates, a lot is at stake. If the student's culturally influenced behavior patterns mesh with his/her classmates', there is no problem. But, if the student exhibits behavior that does not coincide with the new culture, the child is disconcerted by the cultural clash, and his/her self-concept is proportionately diminished. To the extent that the child feels that his/her language and culture are unacceptable in school, which is a reflection of society at large, the child will suffer a loss of self-esteem. S/he may begin to believe that his/her parents, language, and culture are somehow less digni-

---

*Ramirez and Castaneda (1974) list recommendations for implementing culture-matching teaching strategies in their text, *Cultural Democracy, Bicognitive Development, and Education*, New York: Academic Press, 1974.

fied than those of his/her classmates. Because the positive self-concept required for learning is absent, learning is difficult for the student.

Another factor influencing a student's learning style is his/her unique set of values. Thus, the teacher should be aware that the bilingual exceptional child may respond to stimuli differently from other children. For example, because a Spanish-speaking student may value his/her parents' pride in school work more than an Anglo child does, a note sent home stating the child's accomplishments may be more reinforcing for the bilingual special education student than would a tangible or social reward.

PARENT INVOLVEMENT

Public Law 94-142 legitimized the role of parents as participating members of the educational decision team by requiring that parents be informed of, and involved in, all decisions regarding educational testing and placement of their children and by necessitating that such testing and placement procedures consider the native language of both parent and child. However, despite such legislation, minority language parents have been conspicuously nonparticipatory in the schools. Thus, more often than not, the parents of bilingual exceptional children are absent from educational activities, such as parent-teacher conferences, meeting of parent-teacher organizations, and admission, review, and dismissal committees.

One of the reasons that minority language parents often exclude themselves from their children's educational process is, of course, that they feel intimidated by the language barrier. If they do not speak English, these parents are embarrassed by their inability to communicate with school staff and may fear rejection. They may also be inhibited by the institutional setting of the schools. In addition, these parents shy away because they do not know what may be expected of them. Teachers and administrators constantly require additional training in methods of providing required services; therefore, consideration must be given to these parents, who do not speak English and who experience difficulty in understanding and assimilating these changes in trying to seek help for their handicapped children (Bergin, 1979).

Thus, educators of exceptional bilingual students must meet the challenge of involving parents in their children's educational process. Efforts have been made to attack this problem by asking parents to participate in classroom activities related to the child's culture. But, to be effective, an extension of the school's instructional program must be carried out at home. Even more important may be an ongoing relationship between the school program and home support. Informal contact within the student's neighborhood or home may be more desirable than formal parent-teacher conferences in the school. During such relaxed meetings, practical suggestions can be made regarding the day-to-day problems the parents face. And, through counseling, the parent may gain a needed knowledge of special education specific to his/her child's disability.

Finally, organizational efforts may be made. Having addressed those issues which need immediate attention through staff development, research, and cultural awareness, groups such as The Council for Exceptional Children can aid by developing and disseminating bilingual special educational materials, promoting and encouraging research, and hosting conferences and workshops in the area of bilingual special education.

CONCLUSION

Despite the concern of educators over inappropriate assessment and placement procedures of bilingual special education children, this problem continues to exist in our present educational system. As discussed above, these problems can be challenged through more appropriate assessment procedures, cultural awareness training of monolingual teachers, methodology, learning styles, parent involvement, and research concerning the bilingual special education student.

REFERENCES

Bergin, V. *Special Education Needs in Bilingual Programs*. Rosslyn, VA: National Clearinghouse for Bilingual Education, 1979.

Bernal, E. "Assessing Assessment Instruments: A Chicano Perspective." Paper presented at the Regional Training Program to Serve the Bilingual/Bicultural Exceptional Child, Mental Educational Associates, Sacramento, CA, 1972.

Bryen, D.N. "Special Education and the Linguistically Different Child." *Exceptional Children* 40 (8) (May 1974): 589–99.

deAvila, E.A. & Havassy, B. IQ Tests and Minority Children. Austin, TX: Dissemination Center for Bilingual Bicultural Education, 1975.

Dunn, L.M. "Special Education for the Mildly Retarded—Is It Justifiable?" *Exceptional Children* 35 (1) (September 1968): 5–22.

Larry P. vs. W. Riles, in *Opinion* U.S. District Court, Northern District of California, No. C-71-2270 RFP 1979.

Jaramillo, M. "Cultural Conflict Curriculum and the Exceptional Child." *Exceptional Children* 40 (8) (May 1974): 585–88.

Jones, R.L. and Wilderson. "Mainstreaming and the Minority Child: An Overview of the Issues and a Perspective." In *Mainstreaming and the*

Minority Child, edited by R.L. Jones. Reston, VA: The Council for Exceptional Children, 1976.

Mercer, J. "IQ: The Lethal Label." *Psychology Today* 6 (4) (September 1972): 44–77.

Moreno, S. "Problems Related to Present Testing Instruments." In *Voices,* edited by D.I. Romano. Berkeley, CA: Quinta Sol, 1971.

Ortega, F. "Special Education Placement and Mexican-Americans." In *Voices,* edited by D.I. Romano. Berkeley, CA: Quinta Sol, 1971.

President's Committee on Mental Retardation. *MR Priority Report: The Retarded Victims of Poverty.* Washington, DC: U.S. Government Printing Office, n.d.

Ramirez, M. and Castaneda, A. *Cultural Democracy: Bicognitive Development and Education.* New York: Academic Press, 1974.

Reyes, V.H. "Self-Concept and the Bicultural Child." In *Bridging Two Cultures,* edited by M. Cotera and L. Hufford. Austin, TX: National Educational Laboratory Publishers, Inc., 1980.

Reynolds, M. C. and Birch, J.W. *Teaching Exceptional Children In All America's Schools.* Reston, VA: The Council for Exceptional Children, 1977.

Assessing the Bilingual Handicapped Student

by Barbara A. Mowder

Federal legislation demands that bilingual children be assessed in their primary language or mode of communication. This means that bilingual children with possible handicapping conditions must be assessed to determine their dominant language and that further testing must be conducted in their primary mode of communication. This paper explores the issues involved in assessing bilingualism and handicapping conditions (e.g., learning disabilities) of bilingual, culturally different children and evaluates the assessment methods that have been devised.

Both the Education Amendments of 1974 (Public Law 93-380) and the Education for All Handicapped Children Act of 1975 (Public Law 94-142) firmly establish the right of all handicapped children to a free, appropriate, public education, with the goal of providing full educational opportunities for all handicapped children. To receive an appropriate, individualized education, handicapped children must be identified, evaluated, and recommended for educational programs. While the assessment of children with handicapping conditions can be difficult, it is especially hard with bilingual handicapped children, because these children use two languages to varying degrees and few assessment instruments accommodate to this fact. Moreover, many bilingual children have been misclassified as handicapped, an error which has resulted in court cases charging discrimination in educational assessment procedures (e.g., Diana vs. California State Board of Education; Arreola vs. Santa Ana Board of Education). These assessment and evaluation problems were recognized when both Public Laws 93-380 and 94-142 were written, and thus each law contains provisions stating that procedures must be adopted to assure that testing and evaluation materials are selected and administered so as not to be racially or culturally discriminatory. Public Law 94-142 went even further by specifying two more conditions: first, no single assessment instrument may be used as the sole criterion for placement; second, testing must be in the child's native language or mode of communication. Clearly, the necessity of assessing bilingual children with possible handicapping conditions poses several problems for school psychologists, who typically evaluate and make educational recommendations for handicapped children. For instance, school psychologists are typically monolingual and, in addition, no tests have been developed that are totally nondiscriminatory. Furthermore, most psychologists realize that changing tests so that they are in fact nondiscriminatory does not address the real problem—that culturally different children continue to experience failure in a white, middle class educational system, regardless of changes in testing procedures.

BILINGUALISM

Definitions of bilingualism center around a common theme: bilingual individuals make use of two languages. Laosa (1975) recognizes bilingualism whenever a native speaker of one language makes use of a second language, regardless of how partially or imperfectly, and feels that bilingualism ranges from the individual's "seldom use of anything but the native language, through speakers who make use of a second language in varying degrees, to the rarely encountered ambilingual who achieves complete mastery in both languages" (p. 716). Another, similar definition is given by Cornejo (1974), who sees bilingualism as varying "from about 100% monolingual Spanish to about 100% monolingual English, with various degrees in between" (p. 296).

While the number of bilingual individuals in the United States is significant, the number who report a language other than English as their primary language is also substantial. In a report issued July, 1976, the Bureau of the Census (Note 1) reports that over 8.8% of the population four years old and over identify a language other than English as their primary language. This means that more than 17 million individuals use English as a second language. While Spanish is the second most widely used language in the United States following English, many report French, German, Italian, and others as their primary language. Actually, the percentage of bilinguals of elementary and secondary school age (4–17 years) who report languages other than English as their primary language varies within each language group. For instance, only about 5% of persons whose usual language is Italian are of school age, while 21% of those whose usual language is Spanish are of school age. While the Bureau of the Census estimates show that well over one million school children have a primary language other than English, they grossly underestimate the figures of those who are bilingual.

Assessing Bilingualism

Determining the degree of bilingualism and, in fact, the dominant language of the bilingual can be difficult. Assessment instruments must be devised to evaluate a large number of combinations of bilingualism in this country (e.g., English-Spanish, English-Filipino, English-Korean), and these instruments must be attuned to the fact that the degree of bilingualism varies within age groups in each bilingual combination. An overriding factor is that bilingualism varies within the use of any two specific languages; for example, it is erroneous to treat all Spanish-speaking bilinguals as if they formed a homogeneous group. Laosa (1975) notes that there are several distinct Spanish-American groups in the United States (e.g., Central Texas Mexican-Americans, Miami Cuban-Americans, and New York Puerto Ricans), each with quite different cultural, linguistic, and socioeconomic characteristics. Others also have shown how language characteristics of different bilingual groups can obscure the assessment of bilingualism (Matluck & Mace, 1973). Indeed, a further source of variability among bilingual subgroups is not only the degree of bilingualism, but also the contextual use of language.

Laosa (1975) notes that the extent of bilingualism in Spanish-speaking subgroups is due to several variables, among them the duration of contact with the homeland, and social pressures. For instance, New York Puerto Ricans show the greatest degree of maintenance of the mother tongue (Spanish), while the Central Texas Mexican-American groups show the greatest degree of language shift. Furthermore, Laosa demonstrates that subgroups vary in their contextual (e.g., familial, social, school) use of language. He found, for example, that generally Miami Cuban-American and New York Puerto Rican children use their parents' language pattern in the familial context, but that Mexican-American children tend to use a mixture, even if their parents use Spanish at home.

The use of two languages, in various contexts and to various extents, brings up the problem of language borrowing. Although language borrowing affects monolinguals and bilinguals alike in the use of words such as chef and gringo, these elements form a common code; no difficulty ensues when either group uses the elements. But when a bilingual forms a combination of elements from two languages in no commonly accepted code, then interference via language borrowing has occurred. Mackey (1965) finds that interference of one language in the use of another is one of the most obvious effects of bilingualism. He clarifies the issues involved by stating that:

> Interference is the use of elements from one language while speaking or writing another. It is a characteristic of the message, not of the

> code. It varies quantitatively and qualitatively from bilingual to bilingual and from time to time in the same individual, ranging from an almost imperceptible stylistic variation to the most obvious sort of speech mixture. (p. 239)

Language borrowing and interference, for the bilingual, occur in any two-way communication of listening-speaking, listening-writing, reading-speaking, and reading-writing, as well as in one-way communications such as listening to a lecture, praying, or writing in a diary (Mackey, 1965), which makes the assessment problems even more difficult.

Even though the individual bilingual's use of the two languages varies for specific purposes and functions, as well as in different contexts, Hickey (1972) states that there is no theory to explain interference. But many researchers have been investigating this phenomenon and their findings have direct implications for the assessment of bilingualism. Edelman (1969), for instance, tapped proficiency as well as language use in various settings and found that, within the Puerto Rican group he investigated, language proficiency scores were closely tied to usage scores; that is, the more one language is used, the more proficient individuals are, and the less interference occurs.

The assessment of bilingualism is a complex procedure, with many factors that must be considered (e.g., the extent of language borrowing and interference, language use in different contexts). To assess bilingualism itself, it is necessary to determine the linguistic skills that a child has obtained in each language. Matluck and Mace (1973) note several implications for the assessment of bilingual children: first, language use or competency in each language must be evaluated in relation to the child's developmental stage; and second, the bilingual child's language should be compared with the monolinguals of the same developmental level. Therefore, it is important to separate language deviations that are due to developmental processes from those that are due to language inteference. Several further considerations must be mentioned in assessing the bilingual child's language use. Assessment must reflect proficiency within the dialect the child speaks, as well as proficiency in different contexts. Moreover, noting the child's socioeconomic background, parental level of education, and community attitude toward language use plays a role in the accurate assessment of bilingual children's language use and proficiency.

Test instruments must assess use of both languages in various contexts, with a consideration of the child's dialect, socioeconomic, familial, and cultural background. But in choosing or developing test instruments to assess bilingualism, the most important variable is the reason for assessing bilingualism. Assessment functions tend to fall into one of several categories:

1. To determine a bilingual child's dominant language.
2. To diagnose a bilingual child's strengths and weaknesses in both languages.
3. To determine possible placement in language classes.
4. To determine appropriateness of the child for an instructional program.
5. To determine whether further testing, in the child's dominant language, is necessary.

Assessing bilingualism, therefore, can give an indication of whether further language assessments should be carried out, and an idea of the child's strengths and weaknesses in each language. Determining the purpose of testing makes the relative consideration of dialect, socioeconomic, and other factors more clear.

Once the purpose is determined, Matluck and Mace (1973) make specific recommendations for test instruments developed to assess bilingualism; these suggestions fall into three categories—format, content, and supporting material. Format should include separate measures of children's receptive (listening comprehension) and expressive (verbal language) abilities; and the testing method and time requirements should be appropriate to the child's age. Dual measures of language ability are necessary to detect potential differences in the development of listening and speaking skills, and using pictorial stimuli, rather than verbal cues, may be necessary to get an accurate assessment of these abilities in young children. A more general consideration, which is necessary when assessing young children for any reason, is that administration should be within a time frame suitable to a young child. Furthermore, they suggest that the test content should be carefully selected and designed to include items of reasonable linguistic complexity for children's various age levels. In addition, the items should reflect the language usage and cultural patterns of the child's regional dialect. Finally, supporting materials, such as stimulus pictures, should consider the perceptual requirements and the appropriateness of the media (e.g., line drawings, photographs) and the content (e.g., urban experiences, rural experiences) to the child's age, regional, and cultural background.

EXAMINER ISSUES

Once a test to assess bilingualism has been constructed, an examiner must use it to evaluate bilingual children. It would be difficult, at best, for a nonbilingual examiner to conduct the assessment, but even if the examiner is bilingual, problems still may occur. The examiner's dominant language may not be the same as that of the child being assessed, or even if the dominant languages are the same, the dialect, regional, and cultural backgrounds may differ. Beyond these points, though, the examiner and the child may not borrow from their nondominant language to the same extent, nor in the same context. For example, a New York Puerto Rican bilingual psychological examiner may have no further understanding of a Mexican-American child's language than has a monolingual English examiner. Ideally, examiners should be bilingual and thoroughly familiar with the dialect, regional, and cultural background of the children they assess. However, the fact remains that there are insufficient numbers of psychologists with fluency in a second language for this to be a reality.

While Sabatino, Kelling, and Hayden (1973) recommend that institutions of higher education move swiftly to recruit bilingual students for school psychology programs, the fact remains that at present there are insufficient numbers to assess children who are bilingual. While the effects between bilingual language proficiency in the examiner and performance and the evaluation of the child being assessed seem unclear at this point, it is clear that bilingual examiners are necessary to determine bilingual children's language usage. Furthermore, bilingual examiners are necessary to assess children whose dominant language is other than English to determine any handicapping condition.

ASSESSING BILINGUAL HANDICAPPED CHILDREN

Although children must now be assessed in their primary language, how best to assess bilingual and culturally different children for handicapping conditions has long been a puzzle to measurement experts and psychologists. Several different methods have been suggested, among them translating existing tests into different languages, using nonverbal assessment materials, devising criterion-referenced measures, and using behavior rating scales. Although various suggestions have been proposed, the urgency of devising appropriate assessment materials for bilingual children has never been so immediate.

Decisions involving assessment instruments can more easily be made once the testing criticisms are better understood. Sabatino, Kelling, and Hayden (1973) sum up the problems by stating that testing has been biased with respect to minority group children's linguistic, cultural, and socioeconomic backgrounds. Furthermore, they find that tests used to place children in special education programs

> . . . have been generally standardized on white, English-speaking,
> middle class student populations, and furthermore contain many cul-
> turally loaded questions asked in and often requiring answers in

English. In addition, test directions are usually administered in English. Therefore, when such tests are administered to culturally different children, the scores obtained may reflect their unfamiliarity with the dominant culture and the English language. (p. 563)

However, the major problem in assessing bilingual, culturally different children is that the majority of tests used to evaluate intellectual aptitudes and achievement require receptive and expressive language abilities (Oakland & Matuszek, 1976). What seems necessary are assessment instruments that maximize children's ability to understand what is required and to respond comfortably by using their best language abilities, or nonverbal expressive skills. In fact, Cleary, Humphreys, Kendrick, and Wesman (1975) state that no objective measures have been developed to tap the intellectual repertoire of bilingual children. Moreover, they feel that the repertoire can be sampled only by testing in both languages, because abilities in the separate languages will rarely overlap completely. At this point, Cleary, et al., (1975) state "test administrators should assume that either language score standing alone is undoubtedly an underestimate of the bilingual child's current repertoire" (p. 22). At the very least, it seems that assessments should include ways for bilingual children to respond to the best of their abilities, and furthermore that the testing should be in both of the child's languages.

The suggestions for assessing bilingual children for handicapping conditions fall into several groups.

Translating Test Instruments

While some tests have been translated into other languages, and other standardized instruments have developed parallel forms in other languages, this method has numerous pitfalls. In fact, translating a test from English to another language may not remove language biases, it may increase them (Oakland & Matuszek, 1976). Laosa (1976) feels that more than mere translation and superficial adaptation are necessary before a test can be considered appropriately equivalent. DeAvila and Havassy (1974) further enumerate the difficulties with translating existing tests: first, regional linguistic differences make it difficult to use a single translation; second, monolingual translations are inappropriate because a bilingual child's language may be a combination of two languages (e.g., Tex-Mex); and third, many bilingual children do not read in their dominant, spoken language.

Culture Fair Tests

Another trend that has been evident for some time are the efforts that have been directed toward developing culture fair or culture free tests.

These tests were developed to minimize culture specific factors such as language, reading, and speed that affect test content and test-taking behaviors (Laosa, 1976). Examples of culture fair tests include Raven's Progressive Matrices, Cattell's Culture-Fair Intelligence Tests, and the Leiter International Performance Scale. But Oakland and Matuszek (1976) feel the interest in developing culture free tests is declining as psychologists become increasingly aware that one test cannot be universally appropriate to individuals from all cultures, representing all languages, and still assess important psychological characteristics.

Behavior Rating Scales

Some have posited "adaptation to one's environment" as the appropriate way of determining cognitive development, thus supporting the use of behavior rating scales and other observation systems as a measurement of intelligence. But Cleary, et al., (1975) reject this approach, citing two reasons: first, the definition is so broad that it is virtually meaningless for the purpose of criterion development as well as for test use; and second, if the environment is too narrowly defined (e.g., the ability to deal with living in the inner city), the resulting measure has too little generalizability.

Regional Norms

Establishing regional norms is yet another way educators have proposed to reflect more accurately minority children's cognitive and achievement patterns. This means that children's performance is compared with other children in their region or locality, rather than with the white, English-speaking, middle class children who frequently make up the standardization norms. However, while this provides comparisons of children's performance with others within the region, it does not address the major issues of why these children do not perform well on these measures (Laosa, 1976), and why they do not achieve well in school. While Cleary, et al., (1975) call for more normative data to help the educational system and society understand the handicaps under which culturally different individuals must operate, and to help in the selection of tests that are at more appropriate levels of difficulty for the culturally different, DeAvila and Havassy (1974) point out the impracticality of this approach. Devising accurate norms for each region and each subgroup and determining which norms the children would be compared with represent enormous difficulties. Moreover, moving in this direction does not consider the major question that educators must address—once deficits are determined and the differences documented, will it make any difference until the educational system, curriculum, and instruction are modified to accommodate for the differences that bilingual, culturally different children bring to the school?

Criterion-Referenced Measures

One method that departs substantially from past testing practices is the criterion-referenced approach. As opposed to norm-referencing, which compares one child's performance to that of other children, criterion-referenced assessment sets a standard to which each child's performance is compared. Criterion-referenced measures are designed so that children's achievement is evaluated on clearly specified educational tasks. One substantial attempt to develop a criterion-referenced system for evaluating Spanish reading is the SOBER-Espanol (Cornejo, 1974). But Laosa (1976) feels that, while criterion-referenced testing represents a step toward systematic sequencing of learning tasks leading to proficiency in a given subject matter, the method is not free of problems. It seems that developing an accepted set of mastery items would represent few difficulties, but getting consensus on determining the objectives, the behavioral criterion levels, and what constitutes a sufficient sample of criterion levels can be difficult. And, in addition, the test items must be examined to see if they accurately reflect the behavioral criteria, and the test scores must be inspected to determine whether they accurately describe an individual's response pattern (Bohem, 1973).

Pluralistic Assessment Techniques

The most recent approach to the problem of assessing and making recommendations for culturally different children attempts to take into account sociocultural factors when evaluating intelligence aptitude scores. Pluralistic assessment as proposed by Mercer and Lewis (1976) draws on several theoretical models and gives an estimate of bilingual, culturally different children's learning potential. While this method appears to keep children out of special education classes who do not belong there, it fails to address the issue of why a disproportionate number of minority group children score low on general intelligence tests and other measures that are highly correlated with academic criteria and measures of success in school. In other words, while they do seem to sort out handicapped from nonhandicapped children, pluralistic assessment techniques do not offer suggestions for children who perform poorly on standardized assessment instruments and also perform poorly in school.

Some educators point out the deficiencies in current assessment procedures and call for a halt to current testing practices. Others (DeAvila & Havassy, 1974) hold the opinion that tests as they currently are designed are of little use to anyone and therefore their abolition represents little loss. But Meeker and Meeker (1973) point out that the abolition of testing potentially causes greater problems. In fact, they feel that, if educators are denied access to relevant information, they will be forced to make informal assessments subject to just as many, if not more, deficiencies. The problem remains, however, that many bilingual and culturally different children have been misclassified as handicapped and placed in special education programs in numbers disproportionate to their representation in the general population. Moreover, few recognize the fact that these children's scores on the tests do seem to correspond accurately to their school achievement. Thus, while a number of remedies have been proposed to alleviate the symptom—the testing difficulties—few have been proposed to address the problem—that bilingual and culturally different children continue to experience failure in a predominantly white, middle class school system that reflects the majority culture's language and sociocultural values. Cleary, et al., (1975) take the stand that, "It appears likely that until massive educational intervention on behalf of the disadvantaged has taken place, they can be expected to show appreciable deficits, on the average, on present ability tests" (p. 39).

NOTE

1. Bureau of the Census, U.S. Department of Commerce, Language usage in the United States, July, 1975, *Current Population Studies*, July, 1976.

REFERENCES

Bohem, A. E. Criteria-referenced assessment for the teacher. *Teachers College Record*, 1973, *75*, 117–126.

Cleary, T. A., Humphreys, L. G., Kendrick, S. A., & Wesman, A. Educational uses of tests with disadvantaged students. *American Psychologist*, 1975, *30*, 15–41.

Cornejo, R. J. A criterion-referenced assessment system for bilingual reading. *California Journal of Educational Research*, 1974, *25*, 294–301.

DeAvila, E. A., & Havassy, B. The testing of minority children—a neo-Piagetian approach. *Today's Education*, 1974, *63*, 71–75.

Edelman, M. The contextualization of school children's bilingualism. *Modern Language Journal*, 1969, *53*, 179–182.

Hickey, T. Bilingualism and the measurement of intelligence and verbal learning ability. *Exceptional Children*, 1972, *30*, 24–28.

Laosa, L. M. Bilingualism in three U.S. Hispanic groups: Contextual use of language by children and adults in their families. *Journal of Educational Psychology,* 1975, *67,* 617–627.

Laosa, L. M. Historical antecedents and current issues in nondiscriminatory assessment of children's abilities. In *With bias toward none.* Lexington, KY: Coordinating Office of Regional Resource Centers, 1976.

Mackey, W. Bilingual interference: Its analysis and measurement. *Journal of Communication,* 1965, *15,* 239–249.

Matluck, J. H., & Mace, B. J. Language characteristics of Mexican-American children: Implications for assessment. *Journal of School Psychology,* 1973, *11,* 365–386.

Meeker, M., & Meeker, R. Strategies for assessing intellectual patterns in black, Anglo, and Mexican-American boys—or any other children—and implications for education. *Journal of School Psychology,* 1973, *11,* 341–350.

Mercer, J., & Lewis, J. F. A system of multicultural pluralistic assessment (SOMPA). In *With bias toward none.* Lexington KY: Coordinating Office of Regional Resource Centers, 1976.

Oakland, T., & Matuszek, P. Using tests in nondiscriminatory assessment. In *With bias toward none.* Lexington, KY: Coordinating Office of Regional Resource Centers, 1976.

Sabatino, D., Kelling, K., & Hayden, D. Special education and the culturally different child: Implications for assessment and intervention. *Exceptional Children,* 1973, *39,* 563–567.

Curriculum Development for Culturally Different Exceptional Children

by Philip C. Chinn

Culturally different exceptional children represent a special group. Clearly, we must provide unique services to meet their educational needs. These children are unique in themselves, as they can be considered a minority from two different perspectives. First, they are a minority because of their exceptional status, either handicapped or gifted. Secondly, they are a minority by virtue of their cultural diversity.

Cultural diversity itself is a complex issue, as there are a number of viewpoints regarding what constitutes a cultural group. Frequently cultural groups have been described strictly from an ethnic perspective. The ethnic groups within the United States most often identified as culturally diverse have been the Asian-American, the Blacks, Mexican-Americans (Chicanos), Native American Indians, and Puerto Ricans. There are, however, numerous other ethnic groups which could be considered diverse.

In 1977, the National Council for the Accreditation of Teacher Education (NCATE) issued revised standards for accreditation which include multicultural education. Included in Section 2.1.1 on Multicultural Education is the statement that:

> Multicultural education could include but not be limited to experiences which: (1) promote analytical and evaluative abilities to confront issues such as participatory democracy, racism and sexism, and the parity of power; (2) develop skills for values clarification, including the study of the manifest and latent transmission of values; (3) examine the dynamics of diverse cultures and the implications for developing teaching strategies; and (4) examine linguistic variations and diverse learning styles as a basis for the development of appropriate teaching strategies. (p.4)

This statement clearly suggests that the parameters of multicultural education extend beyond ethnic studies. While ethnic studies will likely be a focal point for multicultural education, other groups may be considered cultural groups in our society. Multicultural education may very well be viewed from the standpoint of sex, religion, age, language, handicapping conditions (e.g., the deaf community as a cultural group), and socioeconomic level.

For the purposes of this article, we will view culture from the perspective of ethnic groups with the five previously mentioned groups as a primary concern. As a caution to you, however, there are other groups that do not come under this rubric who warrant special consideration if their educational needs are to be appropriately provided for. The Hasidic Jews, for example, are an ultraconservative group of Jews who are more likely to be viewed as a religious group than an ethnic group. Their unique religious practices set them apart even from other Jewish Americans. The Amish, likewise, are a unique cultural group which is generally classified as a religious group. Their avoidance of many mechanical and modern conveniences and their strict adherence to their religious principles also set this group apart from others. Both of these groups are diverse cultural groups whose beliefs, customs, and cultural values undoubtedly affect the development of any appropriate educational programming for them. As a side note, although the term *culturally diverse* carries with it a more positive connotation, it will be used interchangeably in this paper with *minority*.

SPECIAL CURRICULA FOR CULTURALLY DIFFERENT EXCEPTIONAL CHILDREN

A thorough search of two computer databases, ERIC and ECER, yielded approximately 240 abstracts. Descriptors in the search included *culturally diverse, culturally different, culturally disadvantaged, minority,* each of the five previously identified ethnic groups, *exceptional children,* each area of exceptionality, *curriculum, instructional methods, instructional strategies,* etc. A second search included these two databases and NIMIS to determine if any curricula exist related to ethnic studies or ethnic heritage for mentally retarded culturally diverse children.

The search for general curricula yielded an extremely limited number of program descriptions and suggested instructional strategies, which will be discussed. The search for ethnic studies curricula was fruitless. Essentially, the searches failed to yield curricula related specifically to culturally diverse exceptional children. A few suggestions for teaching strategies and approaches were cited and will be discussed.

The Council for Exceptional Children has a number of publications related to the education of culturally diverse exceptional children. Among these are selected papers from the 1973 CEC Institutes and Conference on

Cultural Diversity and Exceptional Youth; audio tapes related to cultural diversity; a November, 1974, special issue of *Exceptional Children; Discovery and Nurturance of Giftedness in the Culturally Different,* by E. Paul Torrance; and *Mainstreaming and the Minority Child*, edited by Reginald Jones. Torrance suggests some strategies which are unique to gifted culturally diverse children. In general, however, most of the other publications address strategies and curricular adaptations which are appropriate to culturally diverse children but are not necessarily unique to the exceptional culturally diverse.

This absence of literature pertaining to specific curricula and instructional strategies for culturally diverse exceptional children suggests that either they do not exist or that the isolated curricula and strategies that do exist have not been published or disseminated. The reality is probably a little in between. There are few, if any, curricula that have been developed and are available for dissemination. There are few, if any, developed instructional strategies which have universal appeal and utilitarian value. However, there are probably a number of curricula that have been developed by individual teachers designed specifically to meet the needs of their own group of students. Likewise, many teachers have probably developed their own instructional strategies which are appropriate for specific culturally diverse exceptional children. The individual characteristics of these children all but preclude the development of effective cookbook approaches.

WHAT SHOULD BE TAUGHT

In the development of curricula or curricular approaches for culturally diverse exceptional children, there are some specific needs which should be considered. Only after these needs are identified can an effective curriculum be developed. Specific needs will vary from child to child, but there are some general needs which may be applicable to most of these children. Most basic academic as well as nonacademic skills that are programmed for nonminority group children are likely to be of equal value to minority group children. In addition, some areas of special concern may be appropriate to emphasize in developing the curriculum for these children.

We will now look at some topics which should be considered in curriculum development. In addition, as I have suggested (Chinn, 1979), there are many variables which contribute to the social and emotional adjustment of culturally diverse children. Poor adjustment inhibits effective educational programming and all but precludes successful employment adjustment in later years. Among the variables I cite are racism, poverty, health, and the built-in failure system for many culturally diverse children within the educational process.

Ethnic Studies

The inclusion of ethnic studies in the curriculum for all children is a necessity. Ethnic studies for culturally diverse children is absolutely essential. The reasons are numerous and somewhat complex. Nearly all culturally diverse children will encounter some blatant racism throughout their lives. Even those few who are fortunate enough to escape overt racism will encounter the subtle results of racism and stereotyping which depreciate the self-concept of these children. This subtle racism may be difficult to detect, but it is as insidious as overt discrimination.

Labels

One form of subtle racism is the way in which culturally diverse groups are categorized or labeled. The term *minority* itself carries with it a connotation of being less than other groups with respect to power, status, and treatment. Even in situations where a minority group outnumbers other ethnic groups in population size, it may still be relegated to minority status due to the socioeconomic and power structure of the community (Chinn, 1979).

Terms such as *culturally deprived, culturally disadvantaged,* and *culturally different* are frequently used to identify culturally diverse individuals. The first two terms suggest a posture of arrogance, which implies that members of these cultures function at a level below that of the majority group culture. Further, these terms do not recognize the intrinsic value and uniqueness of these cultural groups and their contributions to our society (Chinn, 1979). Even *culturally different* suggests some degree of deviance and carries negative connotations.

Media

The mass media, including newspapers, television, motion pictures, and textbooks, have all contributed to the negative image of culturally diverse individuals either by stereotyping, omissions, or distortions. Stereotyping in movies and television has created distorted views of minority group members. In past years, minorities were almost totally excluded from roles as professionals. Instead they were portrayed in stereotyped, roles. Only in recent years has there been any effort to correct these omissions and stereotypings. The news media continue to support biased reporting. Whites involved in criminal activities seldom are identified by ethnicity—only name, age, and sex—but reports such as "A Black male, age 29, is being held as a suspect . . .'' are typical. This consistent biased reporting may suggest to the community that minority individuals are responsible for most criminal activity.

History books are filled with omissions, distortions, and stereotyping. One prime example is the credit given to engineer Pierre L'Enfant for his role in surveying and designing a master plan for Washington, D.C. Every student who studies the history of Washington or tours the city will be impressed with this man's contributions to American history. The magnificent plaza named in L'Enfant's honor serves as a visible reminder of this man's efforts. Few will read about or hear about the contributions of Benjamin Banneker, a Black, who perhaps played an equally prominent role in the designing of the city. When L'Enfant returned to France with the only set of blueprints, Banneker, who served on the surveying team with L'Enfant, was able to reproduce the plans accurately from memory and facilitated the building of the city. In contrast to the L'Enfant Plaza, only a rather obscure out-of-the-way circle bears Benjamin Banneker's name.

Perhaps the most damaging effect of stereotyping, omissions, and distortions is the negative self-perceptions which are held by many culturally diverse children. Often these children have few positive role models to identify with, either in the home or on the television or movie screen. Consequently, some perceive themselves and their cultural group as inferior to the dominant cultural group. Socially they may perceive themselves as a deviant group. Economically and politically they may view themselves as powerless. Vocationally they are often conditioned to view themselves only qualified as domestic workers, laundrymen, migrant farm workers, or pimps and prostitutes.

Ethnic studies have the potential to develop positive attitudes within both the culturally diverse and the dominant cultural group. Studying diverse cultural groups can help majority group children understand and appreciate differentness. Culturally diverse children can develop a sense of ethnic pride and identity. Carefully developed curricula could rectify much of the negative self-concept that has evolved after years of exposure (for the children and for their parents) to stereotyping, omissions, and distortions through the media.

As we have seen, at the present time there is a conspicuous absence of curricula developed specifically for culturally diverse exceptional children. However, there are a number of ethnic studies curricula available for different level children, covering a wide range of cultural groups. For a number of years Title IX has been funding projects related to curriculum development, training, and dissemination. Presently over 200 of these curricula are housed at the Ethnic Studies Clearinghouse in Boulder, Colorado. They are being catalogued as well as evaluated. Curricula have been developed for all five of the most frequently identified minority groups. In addition, a wide range of curricula for other cultural groups has also been developed. For example, the 56 projects funded for 1978–1979 included the development of curricula for Estonians, Haitians, Hawaiians, Cajun French, and Bulgarians.

Many of these curricula are appropriate for some exceptional children, while others will require various modifications to be useful in special education. But in most instances, the wheel does not need to be reinvented, simply modified to be appropriate to the needs of the student.

Poverty

The disproportionately high numbers of culturally diverse people who live at or below the poverty level is a long-standing phenomenon. Coleman (1976) suggests that nearly a third of the Blacks live in poverty, which is three times greater than for Whites. The ratio for Mexican-Americans (Chicanos) is approximately the same. Poverty is not limited to these groups alone. Many immigrants who do not have the skills to enter into the competitive job market are exploited or receive below-minimum wages. The effects of poverty are potentially devastating.

While the pressures and problems associated with poverty are obvious to anyone who has gone through periods of financial stress, poverty in itself may not be as critical as poverty coupled with the individual's feelings of hopelessness. In times past, immigrants survived the early years of poverty with the anticipation of a better future. Many culturally diverse individuals today, however, see little hope of escape from their way of life. Some find the job market closed to them in spite of their educational achievements. The barriers are still up. While some Americans were generally encouraged with the drop in the unemployment figures released in the spring of1979, there was little room for rejoicing in the Black community. In January, 1979, White unemployment dropped from 5.1 to 4.9%. At the same time, Black unemployment rates rose from 11.2 to 11.9 percent. Unemployment in Black America is now 243% times the rate for the White community; it is nothing short of a social disaster (Rowan, 1979).

The potential effect of poverty has frequently been cited as a factor in aggressive behavior and emotional disturbance. Levine and Kahn (1974) examined 1,000 downtown New York families to determine the relationship between psychological disadvantage and socioeconomic status. They found that lower socioeconomic status and minority ethnic group status were associated with high levels of psychiatric impairment. Frustration leads to despair, anger, aggression, and other deviant behavior, including suicide. Disproportionately high numbers of suicides have been observed among the Chinese in San Francisco and among Native Americans (Chinn, 1973a; Pepper, 1976).

The curriculum for culturally different exceptional children living in poverty situations should include some topics which may never totally alleviate the condition but can make their lives more tolerable. Among the areas of study should be instruction on how to live within the system. That is, how can these individuals learn to live within a system that can provide certain types of government services for those at poverty income levels. Curriculum should include, but not be limited to, instruction about the resources available for food assistance and health care. Even more critical is providing specific information on how to deal with bureaucratic red tape and the numerous obstacles which stand in the way of qualifying for services. Often there are stringent rules and regulations with little assistance or sympathy available for those who are not familiar with the system. Often, even the more capable individuals are discouraged and give up even though they are entitled to services. Culturally different exceptional individuals who have cognitive limitations may need specific help in overcoming their own deficiencies and dealing with intimidating behavior on the part of government officials.

A second area which needs to be strongly emphasized among economically limited students is the use and handling of finances. Special education teachers have long provided EMR students with instruction in this area. With low income, minority students this is equally, if not more, critical. They need to learn the best use of their limited incomes. Among the many areas to be studied are how to budget and how and where to shop, how to find housing, how to borrow money, and how to make installment purchases. With limited financial resources and inflation, they must learn to efficiently use what little they do have.

With the disproportionately high numbers of culturally diverse individuals identified among the ranks of the unemployed, career education appears to be critical for the children in this group. Vocational education should be a critical area of curriculum emphasis, and the development of vocational skills must begin early in the educational process. Other aspects of career education such as leisure skills are also critical areas for curriculum development.

Health

Health problems are frequently associated with poverty; and poverty, as previously cited, is associated with minority groups. Problems center around poor nutrition, poor medical service (typically government-supported), and poor prenatal care. The high incidence of children born at risk (preterm and postterm) to parents of low socioeconomic status has been documented (Kernek, Osterud, & Anderson, 1966). Further, the incidence of brain injury, mental retardation, and learning disabilities has been related to children born at risk. These problems are directly related to the school problems so frequently identified with children from minority groups. Tarnopol (1970) found that minority group children had a significant degree of minimal brain damage related to learning disabilities. He suggests that delinquency and dropping out of school by minority group children may be partially related to brain dysfunction.

In a study comparing the physical well-being of third grade students as determined by a physical examination, Chinn (1973b) found a direct relationship between physical well-being and teacher ratings of the student's academic performance and social acceptance by peers. The poor health conditions of some culturally diverse students may affect their functional abilities in school.

Curricular adaptations for culturally diverse exceptional children may include information regarding access to government medical and dental care. Also, instruction on good health care procedures for themselves and their families should be an integral part of the curriculum.

Education

To the average middle-class child, school is a highly valued institution. The influences of parents, siblings, and other people in the child's environment lead to positive perceptions of school. Most children see it as a place where learning takes place; where learning is an enjoyable experience. School is also viewed as a positive social institution where the child is valued by his teachers and his peers (Chinn, 1979).

Disillusioned by their educational experiences, many minority group parents view school from a more negative perspective, and older children often share the same perceptions. Minority group children frequently begin school with little enthusiasm; for other people in their world, the school is an institution which represents failure, frustration, rejection, and at times discrimination. Too often their preconceived ideas are justified (Chinn, 1979).

The drop-out rate for minority students is alarming. About 800,000 students drop out of school each year. Twenty-two out of every 100 students who enter the fifth grade do not complete high school. Garcia (1976) reports that 45% of Mexican-American children drop out before completing the twelfth grade. The attrition rate for Native Americans is 55%. Of the dropouts, 85% are poor Blacks and Hispanics, along with poor Whites. In larger cities, the majority of the dropouts are Black, economically disadvantaged youth who have values and attitudes that are incongruent with those of the urban middle class. Many suffer from educational handicaps rooted in their poverty, deprivation, discrimination, and environmental conditions over which they personally have little or no control. In many instances, their home environments do not provide the self-concept, opportunity, motivation, or the capacity to cope with their problems (Jones, 1977).

Cultural Pluralism

In 1908, Zangwill's play *The Melting Pot* saw all of the American people (particularly those of European descent) melting together in God's crucible and then emerging as a new race—as Americans. While the original melting pot concept applied to Europeans, this concept—assimilation—has prevailed. Many teachers are assimilationists who see immigrants and minority group members embracing and being absorbed into the culture, values, and language of the dominant society. In essence, a true assimilationist would have all individuals becoming as close as possible to being White Anglo-Saxon Protestants. They would, in particular, have all Americans use the same language—standard American English.

The 1974 Civil Rights Commission estimated that there were 5,000,000 linguistically different children in the United States. This figure does not include the millions of Black children who use Ebonics (Black English) as their primary medium of communication. The extreme assimilationist would have all these children develop standard English skills to the point of ridding themselves of any traces of non-English languages and nonstandard English dialects. The assimilationist would have immigrants and minority group members rid themselves of their unique characteristics, to become as much as possible "model Americans."

The advocates of the melting pot theory have been effective, to a certain extent. Most European immigrants have been well assimilated in the cultural mainstream. Assimilated minorities have more doors opened to them in occupations, professions, and in other reward systems. The result has been that some Blacks, Asians, Hispanics, and Native Americans are as much a part of the dominant society as that society has allowed them to be. These individuals see assimilation as a vehicle to acceptance and success within the dominant society. Yet in spite of their efforts to embrace the new culture and to become educated, jobs are often still not available at higher echelons, and salaries are disproportionately lower. In spite of their education and cultural sophistication, they still experience social and vocational rejection (Chinn, 1979).

For these people, problems with self-identity often emerge. No longer are they a part of the ethnic community they have rejected, nor are they an integral part of the dominant society. Instead they exist between two worlds. Children who are in the process of breaking from their parents' culture often feel guilty because they are rejecting the family values. They may feel alienated from their family unit and ethnic community and rejected by the dominant group (Chinn, 1979).

Of course, self-imposed assimilation is a matter of choice and is not in itself wrong or particularly undesirable. However, assimilationist views imposed by others on the culturally diverse child negating the value of the child's culture can only be seen as racist.

In the early and middle 1960s, the languages of culturally diverse children (e.g., Ebonics, pidgin English) were viewed as deficiencies. In more recent years, however, the language of these children has been recognized as being different rather than deficient. For instance, Hurley (1975), Cazden (1972), and Houston (1971) all have found that Black English possesses all the characteristics of any language system. Linguistically different children generally fall into one of two categories. There are large numbers of children who speak a nonstandard English dialect such as Hawaiian pidgin or Black English. Other linguistically different children come from homes where the native language is not English (e.g., Chinese, Spanish). From a legal and moral standpoint, this second group of children has received some attention of educators, who use the child's home language as a medium of instruction. This is part of bilingual education. Even though many issues in bilingual education are debatable, the legal rights of these linguistically different children have been provided for in the courts.

Nonstandard English dialects have not enjoyed the same level of support. They do not have legal support, nor do educators agree about whether or not to use these dialects in instruction. In some respects, some individuals from these cultural groups are "bilingual." They use standard English, or an approximation of it, within the educational system, with teachers, majority group peers, and authority figures. Within their own cultural groups, they use the nonstandard English dialect. The use of nonstandard English dialects as a medium of instruction is debatable, and there is not room to address that issue in this paper. What is critical, however, is that educators are aware of the implications of requiring culturally diverse children to use standard English in the classroom. This requirement may have considerable merit in that these children can learn to function linguistically in two worlds, the dominant cultural group and their own. The ability to assimilate linguistically may open social and vocational doors. However, educators should realize that, while the children are learning to function in a different linguistic style, refraining from the use of the child's own cultural group language may keep the child from completely and freely expressing all of his thought patterns. More simply, the child's limited standard English skills may not be as developed as his cognitive skills, and his language limitations may cause the child to appear dull.

Educationally, it is critical that teachers realize that there is no one model American and that the strength of American society exists in a pluralistic culture. The Commission on Multicultural Education of the American Association of Colleges for Teacher Education developed a policy statement adopted in 1972 entitled "No One Model American." As the text states:

> To endorse cultural pluralism is to endorse the principle that there is no one model American. To endorse cultural pluralism is to understand and appreciate the differences that exist among the nation's citizens. It is to see these differences as a positive force in the continuing development of a society which professes a wholesome respect for the intrinsic worth of every individual. Cultural pluralism is more than a temporary accommodation to placate racial and ethnic minorities. It is a concept that aims toward a heightened sense of being and of wholeness of the entire society based on the unique strengths of each of its parts.

The teacher who accepts the basic tenants of this statement will likely be prepared to provide students with appropriate ethnic studies in their curriculum. The same teacher will likely provide or try to provide for the linguistic differences that any of the children may have. Legally, according to laws and court decisions such as the Lau vs. Nichols case (1974), Public Law 94-142, and Section 504, the linguistic needs of these children must be met. More important, however, is that the programming be motivated by feelings of propriety and rightfulness rather than legal compliance.

EXCEPTIONAL CHILDREN

Strategies for Culturally Diverse Gifted and Talented

In adapting the work of Greer and Rubinstein (1972), Frasier, Fisher, and Clinton (1977) suggest that, in developing an appropriate curriculum for culturally diverse gifted children, four key dimensions should be considered: (1) what I want to teach, (2) what I want to learn, (3) what you want to learn, and (4) what you want to teach. Out of these four dimensions emerges a fifth, what we discover together.

In Dimension 1, what I want to teach, the teacher's decisions are based on diagnosis of the children's strengths and weaknesses based on both objective measures and subjective observations. Here are some considerations for working with culturally diverse gifted children. These children:

1. Are capable of operating at higher levels of thought (i.e., analysis, synthesis, evaluation).
2. May need some time in developing lower level thought processes (i.e., knowledge, comprehension, evaluation).
3. Exhibit some nonstandard abilities.
4. May need support in initial exploratory opportunities.
5. Need to have strengths emphasized and weaknesses developed.
   (Baldwin, 1973; Frasier, et al., 1977)

Dimension 2 suggests that the teacher can also learn. The culturally diverse children sometimes bring information into the learning environment in nontraditional ways.

Dimension 3 considers what the learner views as important. This approach is congruent with the view that intrinsic motivation stimulates the learning process.

Dimension 4, which is related to Dimension 3, suggests that what the child wants to *teach* is also an integral part of the learning process.

Dimension 5 is a mutually benefitting experience where all in the learning environment can learn and grow together.

Baldwin (1973) suggests using simulation games, research through films, interviews, and computer-assisted instruction. Baldwin further emphasizes the importance of creative thinking (e.g., elaborative thinking, fluent thinking, and flexible thinking).

Torrance (1977) developed a list of 18 "creative positives" (e.g., fluency and flexibility in figural media), which are sets of characteristics he believes can assist in identifying strengths and giftedness among culturally different students. He contends that these creative positives exist to a higher degree among culturally different groups. The creative positives may be detected by tests, observation of behavior, performance, constructions, or any other means whatsoever. These abilities, Torrance states, "for the most part . . . can be observed with a high degree of frequency among culturally different students by anyone who is willing to become a sensitive, open-minded human being in situations where trust and freedom are established." Torrance further contends that the creative positives can be used to motivate learning, select learning experiences, and develop career plans. In his monograph he provides suggestions and examples on how they might be utilized in the classroom.

Culturally Diverse Retarded Children

Hurley (1975) suggests that, while there is increasing concern about the misplacement of children in special education classes, the fact remains that a sizeable percentage of the special education population is culturally different. To better meet the needs of the culturally different in classes for the retarded, Hurley suggests that certain approaches may be used. One approach suggested is the inductive approach. In the learning processes, the child should not only learn facts, skills, and concepts, but also learn how to learn. The student must learn how to process information which he collects. To do so requires practice, an essential element in the inductive process.

Hurley (1975) cautions that some children may have linguistic limitations even in their nonstandard dialects. Thus the teacher must accommodate and meet the needs of both groups—those limited in standard English as well as those limited in both standard as well as nonstandard dialects. This accommodation may involve reading material. Hurley suggests using the experience story. Here the child dictates from his own perceptions and experiences. This may in some instances be a viable approach to reading for those for whom the regular readers hold minimal interest value.

Learning Characteristics of Culturally Diverse Children

A number of characteristics of culturally diverse children have been identified. These traits in some instances set them apart from the middle-class white child. Some of these characteristics are applicable to a particular group, while others cut across a greater number of groups. Differences in cultures are apt to be more striking among lower-class members of an ethnic group, because they tend to be less assimilated than those who are middle class.

Many educators make the erroneous assumption that culturally diverse children lived in a cultural vacuum before they entered school. In truth, often it is the school which fails to match its methods and curriculum to the child's language, cultural background, and learning style. But when the school fails, the child is regarded as deficient. Black mothers, for example, tend to be more firm and physical in discipline than white mothers. When Black children have white teachers who practice what they have learned in college, the children become uncontrollable and are labeled *discipline problems*.

The differences in white and minority group values can make the educational experience one of cognitive dissonance. For instance, Black, Mexican-American, and Native-American children are often more expressive in the affective domain than white students. Their white peers, however, value the cognitive functioning which the schools value and stress (Burgess, 1978).

Open education settings, designed for the white, middle-class child, are another factor in cultural dissonance. Many Black children perform poorly using educational hardware. The technology and automation which replaces certain interactions between teachers and students creates problems for Black and Mexican-American children who are accustomed to associating learning with the interpersonal interaction found in their family settings.

With regard to cognitive style, Ramirez, Casteneda, and Herold (1974) suggest that Mexican-American children are more field dependent in their perceptions than their Anglo peers. Field dependence related to cognitive style may be a function of how traditional a group is. Traditional groups may be more field dependent, while acculturated groups are more field independent (Hsi & Lim, 1977). Ramirez and his associates (1974) found a greater degree of field dependence among children in communities where social conformity is stressed.

Anderson (1977) states that there are two types of cognitive styles, analytic or abstract and nonanalytic or concrete. School related activities and IQ tests rely heavily on analytic cognitive abilities. Minority group children, particularly Black, Mexican-American and Puerto Rican, tend to manifest the nonanalytic style of cognitive functioning. While developmental psychologists usually consider analytic style as superior to the nonanalytic, and see the latter as indicative of cognitive deficit, others (e.g., Bernstein, 1971) do not view nonanalytic thinking as a *lack* of analytic thinking. Rather, they view it as a positively different form of cognitive functioning. Cognitive style may be a function of socialization typical of an ethnic group.

Anderson (1977) suggests that no group of children can be said to have cognitive deficit in an absolute sense. The ability to perform cognitively may be more a function of experience and the context of the situation in which a culturally diverse child is expected to perform. In testing situations, these children are placed in what Labov (1972) refers to as "an asymmetrical situation where anything he says can be held against him." Anderson (1977) further suggests that teachers erroneously interpret brief communication breakdowns as evidence of cognitive deficits.

CONCLUSION

I have included here only a brief description of some of the learning styles and characteristics of culturally diverse children. This last section is not related specifically to exceptional children, but to culturally diverse children in general. The special educator concerned with providing for the needs of culturally diverse children will find an abundance of literature on this subject.

Special educators have developed, through necessity, the ability to adapt and extract from existing materials. For the culturally diverse, the principles remain the same. Identify the needs of your children, and adapt or modify existing materials with a special education emphasis to meet the needs of the children.

The challenge is there for all educators. If school achievement of culturally diverse exceptional children is to improve, traditional approaches designed for Anglo students must be replaced by alternative approaches tailored to the individual learning styles of each child.

REFERENCES

Anderson, K. M. *Cognitive style and school failure*. Paper presented at the symposium "Anthropology in Institutional Settings," Society for Applied Anthropology and Southwestern Anthropological Association, San Diego, April 6, 1977. (ERIC Document #ED 151 253).

Baldwin, A. Instructional planning for gifted disadvantaged children. *National Leadership Institute, Teacher Education/Early Childhood.* Storrs: University of Connecticut, 1973.

Bernstein, B. *Class, codes and control*. London: Routledge and Kegan Paul, 1971.

Burgess, B. J. Native American learning styles. In L. Morris, G. Sather, & P. Scull (Eds.), *Extracting learning styles from social/cultural diversity*. Washington, D.C.: Southwest Teacher Corps Network, 1978.

Cazden, C. B. *Child language and education*. New York: Holt, Rinehart and Winston, 1972.

Chinn, P.C. The Asian American: a search for identity. In L. Bransford, L. Baca, & K. Lane (Eds.), *Cultural diversity and the exceptional child*. Reston, VA.: The Council for Exceptional Children, 1973.(a)

Chinn, P. C. A relationship between health and school problems: A nursing assessment. *Journal of School Health*, 1973, *43*, 85-89.(b)

Chinn, P. C. *Variables affecting deviant behavior in culturally diverse adolescents*. Paper presented at the First Annual Nebraska Symposium on Current Issues in Educating the Early Adolescent with Severe Behavior Disorders, Omaha, May 10, 1979.

Coleman, J. C. *Abnormal psychology and modern life*, 5th ed. Glenview, IL: Scott, Foresman, 1976

Commission on Multicultural Education. *No one model American*. Washington, D.C.: American Association for Colleges of Teacher Education, 1972.

Frasier, M., Fisher, A., & Clinton, O. R. *Help for organizing productive experiences for culturally diverse gifted and talented*. Paper presented at the Annual International Convention, The Council for Exceptional Children, Atlanta, April 15, 1977. (ERIC Document #ED 141 981).

Garcia, R. L. *Learning in two languages*. Bloomington, Ind.: Phi Delta Kappa Educational Foundation, 1976.

Greer, M., & Rubenstein, B. *Will the real teacher please stand up? A primer in humanistic education*. Pacific Palisades, Calif.: Goodyear, 1972.

Houston, S. H. A reexamination of some assumptions about the language of the disadvantaged child. In S. Chess & A Thomas (Eds.), *Annual progress in child psychiatry and child development*. New York: Brunner/Mazel, 1971.

Hsi, V., & Lim, V. *A summary of selected research on cognitive and perceptual variables*. Berkeley, Calif.: Asian-American Bilingual Center, 1977. (ERIC Document #ED 145 003).

Hurley, O. L. Strategies for culturally different children in classes for the retarded. In E.L. Meyen, G.A. Vergason, & R.J. Whelan (Eds.), *Alternatives for teaching exceptional children*. Denver: Love Publishing, 1975.

Jones, W.M. Impact on society of youth who drop out or are under-educated. *Educational Leadership*. 1977, *34*, 411–416.

Kernek, C., Osterud, H., & Anderson, B. Patterns of prematurity in Oregon. *Northwest Medicine*, 1966, *65*, 639.

Labov, W. The logic of non-standard English. In P.P.G. Giglioli (Ed.), *Language and social concept*. London: Penguin Press, 1972.

Lau vs. Nichols, 414 U.S. 563-572 (January 21, 1974).

Levine, A.S., & Kahn, M.B. Does city living damage kids' minds? *Social and Rehabilitation Record*, 1974, *1*, 25–27.

Pepper, F. C. Teaching the American Indian in mainstream settings. In R.L. Jones (Eds.), *Mainstreaming and the minority child*. Reston, Va.: The Council for Exceptional Children, 1976.

Ramirez, M., Casteneda, A., & Herold, P. The relationship of acculturation to cognitive style among Mexican-Americans. *Journal of Cross-Cultural Psychology*, 1974, *5*, 212–220.

Tarnopol, L. Delinquency and minimal brain dysfunction. *Journal of Learning Disabilities*, 1970, *3*, 200–207.

Rowan, C.T. Black unemployment is society's shame. *The Washington Star*, March 16, 1979. P. A-11.

Torrance, E. P. *Discovery and nurturance of giftedness in the culturally different*. Reston, VA: The Council for Exceptional Children, 1977.

Social and Emotional Needs of Culturally Diverse Children

by Ronald W. Henderson

Teachers and administrators are now well accustomed to being admonished that schools must do a better job of meeting the special needs of children from socially and culturally diverse backgrounds. The prevailing assumption behind this advice seems to be that if children differ culturally from the white, middle class dominated traditions of the schools, their needs must also differ. Thus, for example, educators are advised to match instructional strategies to the cognitive styles that are assumed to differentiate culturally diverse children from their Euro-American peers.

The consequences of following this advice are not clear. While some attempts to match instruction to different cultural styles have been reported as successful, other attempts have produced effects opposite to the hypothesized benefits of instructional matching (Kagan & Buriel, 1977). Moreover, the research base upon which the notion that ethnic groups differ along such cognitive style dimensions as field dependence/independence does not provide entirely consistent results (Knight, Kagan, Nelson, & Gumbiner, 1978). Similarly, inconclusive findings have been reported for such developmental characteristics as self esteem (Gray-Little & Applebaum, 1979) and locus of control (Knight, et al., 1978). In brief, while there is wide agreement that instruction should take culturally determined characteristics into consideration in order to reduce the undesirable effects of discontinuities between home and school learning, there is disagreement about the nature of the differences, their distribution within given groups, and how instruction should be adapted to take these factors into account.

If scientific information concerning the specific nature of cognitive needs among culturally diverse groups of children served by the schools is something less than definitive, knowledge of conditions required to promote their social and emotional well-being is even less clear. It seems unlikely that the basic needs of culturally diverse children vary on the basis of differences in their social and cultural characteristics. Rather it appears that a variety of social and cultural factors interact in ways that serve to curtail the probability that these needs will be met adequately within the context of schooling as presently constituted. While social scientists have shown a long standing interest in the ways in which sociocultural factors influence development, efforts to sort out the influences of complexly intertwined factors have been frustrated by both methodological and definitional problems.

Some of the problems that cloud the understanding of these interactions will be reviewed in this article, and a path model of reciprocal influences will be proposed with implications for the social and emotional well being of children whose cultural background deviates from the implicit expectations of the schools. Social and emotional well-being is too broad and ill defined a set of variables with which to explore the path model hypothesis. Therefore a more restricted aspect of social and emotional adjustment, functional adaptation, will serve to focus the premise explored in the latter portion of the article.

CULTURAL DIVERSITY AND STEREOTYPES
Basic Concepts

The terms *culture* and *society* are used in varied and often undefined ways by social scientists and educators. In their examination of uses of the concept of culture, Kroeber and Kluckhohn (1952) found over 160 definitions of the term in the social science literature. What most of the definitions had in common was the idea that culture is composed of habitual patterns of behavior that are characteristic of a group of people. Those shared behavioral patterns are transmitted from one generation to the next through symbolic communication (Kroeber & Kluckholm, 1952) and through modeling and demonstration (Henderson & Bergan, 1976). Culture includes the goals and values that serve to instigate behavior and determine priorities within a social group.

While British anthropologists use the term society to designate the concept that most American social scientists call culture (Evans-Prichard, 1951; Radcliffe-Browne, 1957), Americans generally use the term society to designate an aggregation of individuals who live together in an organized population (Linton, 1936). Thus, *society* refers to a collective of people while *culture* focuses on the customary behaviors that are shared among people in the group. The terms are often used interchangeably when it is not considered important to distinguish between an aggregate of people and their customary patterns of behavior. The temptation to avoid making this conceptual distinction probably accounts for the popularity of the more general term, *sociocultural*.

People of differing statuses within a society play various roles, and the total set of roles make up the social structure of that group. These roles include those that define social stratification within a society.

The United States is a complex society in which a number of diverse groups may be identified. The members of any of these groups display a distinct way of life and social scientists often designate the group as a subculture. Valentine (1968, cited in Laosa, in press) has noted that the variety of units to which distinctive life ways have been attributed include such diverse groupings as ethnic collectives, socioeconomic strata, age groups, and regional populations. From this perspective it is certainly possible to talk about the subculture of public education as well. But subcultures are distinct from the larger culture only in the limited sense that any part may be distinguished from the whole in which it is embedded (Laosa, in press), and it is in this limited sense that, for lack of a better designation, educators often refer to children who are members of identifiable groups—whose life ways deviate in certain ways from the dominant pattern—as *culturally diverse,* the term employed in this discussion.

Stereotypes

The pitfalls involved in distinguishing the influences of socialization experiences in a subculture are not easy to avoid, even by researchers who are aware of them. During the 1960's educators were introduced to studies that described the cultural characteristics of various ethnic groups. It was assumed that this information would help teachers to acquire a better understanding of the pupils in their charge. While every subculture group is characterized by substantial heterogeneity (Laosa, in press), that diversity was largely ignored and stereotyped views were conveyed. For instance, motivational problems with Black children were attributed, in part, to a matriachal family structure (Moynihan, 1967), a pattern that is less pervasive than the generalizations would suggest (English, 1974). Similarly, male dominance was seen as a hindrance to independence, mobility, and achievement among Mexican American youth (Heller, 1966); yet more recent work among migrant farm labor families found the most common mode of decision making to be egalitarian (Hawks & Taylor, 1975).

A number of studies have reported on the motivational characteristics of children from minority backgrounds. For example, the belief system of Hispanic Americans has been described as highly fatalistic (Heller, 1966; Madsen, 1964; Paz, 1961), a characteristic that has been blamed for hampering educational, social, and economic advancement. Yet when

Farris and Glenn (1976) compared fatalism among Anglos and Mexican Americans in a Texas sample, they found no differences between the groups when they controlled for level of education.

Given findings that have helped to dispel cultural stereotypes, it should be remembered that in most ways members of subcultures within United States society are culturally more similar to each other than they are different, and in most cases within group variation exceeds between group variations. The world of subcultures is one of overlapping distributions.

Methodological Problems

In an ideal world it should be possible to distinguish between the influences of various intertwined cultural and social structural variables. Many studies that compare ethnic or racial minority and nonminority children fail to control for socioeconomic status (Laosa, in press). Thus the results are ambiguous at best and usually misleading. Chan and Rueda (1979) rightly argued that researchers should be careful to distinguish between the effects of poverty and culture in their analyses, but that is more easily said than done. There is little research available on the social or emotional development of ethnic minority children that has accomplished such separation with clarity. Chan and Rueda (1979) made the point that poverty mediates both biomedical health and the socialization environment. Their point is especially well taken with reference to health, but the distinction begins to get more vague when the socialization environment is discussed. For example, they attributed lack of socialization information among the poor to their reliance on the electronic media rather than books, which may be considered an expensive luxury. It is at least as reasonable to attribute this pattern to culturally patterned preferences and values as to poverty in itself.

The difficulty of making clear distinctions between cultural and social structural influences is important because a disproportionate number of children who are from minority group subcultures are also poor. Not all minority children are poor, and not all poor children are minorities. However, poor children, whether minority or not, may display culturally acquired behavior that deviates from the expectations implicit in the culture of the school. To the extent that this is true, they also may be considered ''culturally diverse'' for purposes of the present discussion.

Social and Emotional Well-Being

Problems of social and emotional well-being for culturally diverse children may be examined in a number of alternative ways. For example, as a result of discontinuities between home and school, many culturally diverse children encounter aversive experiences at school that could be explained by conditioning principles. The approach selected for present purposes is to focus on a specific aspect of social competence. The term *social competence* has an appealing ring to it, but as many observers have commented (Anderson & Messick, 1974; Zigler & Trickett, 1978), experts are far from agreement on the meaning of that construct. Recent work (Monson, Greenspan & Simeonsson, 1979) has conceptualized social competence with reference to interpersonal functioning in social settings such as classrooms. Dimensions of this conceptualization that have been examined include interest, curiosity, or assertiveness and conformity to rules and expectations (Kohn & Rosman, 1972; Monson, Greenspan & Simeonsson, 1979). These conceptions are compatible with Laosa's (1979) position that social competence involves functional adaptations to specific environments. Each environment may have its own specific demand characteristics for functional adaptation, and for a child success in two different environments may depend on the degree of overlap in the demand characteristics of the environments (Laosa, 1979).

Within the school environment, demand characteristics to which functional adaptations are required include such behaviors as appearing interested in school work, paying attention, and persisting at tasks. The present discussion focuses on the possible consequences for culturally diverse children who are unable to make a functional adaptation to the interpersonal setting of the school. But implicitly, the conceptualization presented here assumes that a condition required for primary prevention is for educators to know something about the child's environmental organization (Laosa, 1979) and to make adaptations in the interpersonal environment of the classroom that will enable the child to adapt to the requirements of school culture.

A PATH MODEL FOR CHILDREN AT RISK

A substantial body of research reviewed by Brophy and Good (1974) shows quite uniformly that teachers hold differential expectations regarding the academic performance of children who vary in personal characteristics such as sex, age, ethnicity, race, and even physical attractiveness (Brophy & Good, 1974; Henderson, in press). It could be argued that these expectancies are based on actual knowledge of children's motivation and achievement characteristics, but it is instructive to note that teachers may express stereotyped expectations based upon labels assigned to children even when the objective behavioral evidence runs contrary to those expectations.

This point is illustrated in a study (Foster & Ysseldyke, 1976) in which teachers viewed a videotape of a normal fourth grade boy engaged in various test taking and free play activities. Different groups of teachers who viewed the tapes were told that the child whose behavior was depicted on the tape suffered from a different disorder: emotional disturbance, learning disability, or mental retardation. One group of viewers was informed that the child was normal. After viewing the tape, teachers expressed negative expectancies consistent with the deviance label they had been given. Differential expectations were expressed in spite of the fact that the behavior they witnessed was inconsistent with the label.

While the subjects in this study were not minority group children, the results seem particularly relevant to circumstances involving culturally diverse children, because these children have been so heavily over-represented among those to whom deviance labels have been assigned (Richardson, 1979), and a number of studies have been demonstrated that teacher expectations tend to be lower for minority than for majority children. The obvious question to ask, then, is whether or not variations in expectations are associated with differential behavior toward students. The answer seems to be yes.

Research reviewed by Good and Brophy (1974) revealed a fairly uniform pattern showing that whenever investigators have looked for differential treatment of students who vary in sex, achievement, or socioeconomic status, they have found it. An examination of the nature of these differences suggests that teacher communications toward children from lower socioeconomic status and/or racial and ethnic minority backgrounds is more likely to be aimed at controlling or managing behavior than is the case for their peers. Communications to majority, middle class children, in contrast, are more likely to be relevant to the content or skills of instruction than those teacher behaviors that are directed to children from culturally diverse backgrounds (Henderson, in press; Laosa, 1977).

While there is little direct information on the specific effects of differential teacher behaviors on the school achievement of culturally diverse children, an accumulation of research results does establish the general case that level of student involvement in academic tasks and the nature of teacher-student interactions are consistently related to achievement (Hoge & Luce, 1979). These findings are of particular interest when viewed in relationship to research on locus of control and learned helplessness, which provides a theoretical framework to explain how differences in teacher expectancies and interaction patterns may affect both the socioemotional development and achievement patterns of children with diverse socialization experiences outside the school.

PERCEPTIONS OF PERSONAL EFFICACY

Locus of Control

Locus of control is a personality construct that refers to the tendency of different individuals to perceive the events that influence their lives either as the consequence of their own actions (internal control) or as the result of external forces beyond their influence (external control). There is generally a positive relationship between internal perceptions of control and academic achievement (Henderson, in press; Lefcourt, 1976). Minority and poor children tend to score more toward the external end of the scale than their nonminority and more affluent peers (Henderson & Bergan, 1976).

Attribution Theory

Differences in locus of control have been explained on the basis of learned expectancies of reward as a consequence of behavior (Rotter, 1966), but more recently Heider's attribution theory (Weiner, 1979) has been used to amplify conceptions of locus of control and the closely related concept of learned helplessness. Individuals who find themselves unable to control aversive stimuli to which they are exposed often come to perceive themselves as helpless. Where the aversive experience is failure at a task that such individuals believe to be important, they may come to see themselves as incapable of overcoming failure. Failure leads to anxiety and deterioration of performance. Following failure experiences these individuals are likely to perform unsuccessfully even on tasks at which they were previously proficient. Children who experience repeated failure at the tasks assigned to them at school are likely to come to perceive themselves as incapable of accomplishing other tasks of the same kind. If the cognitive skills and behavioral norms a child has learned in the subculture of the home differ from those the school culture is prepared to build on, a disproportionate number of such children are likely to experience failure that is beyond their control and subsequently they will come to attribute failure to inability.

Causality may be attributed to a number of internal factors such as ability or effort, or to external factors such as luck or task difficulty (Heider, 1958). For example, an individual may perceive success or failure at a task as the result of ability (or inability) or level of effort. Within the norm referenced world of the classroom, children may be unable to discern their progress in relation to their own past performance, because implicit and explicit comparisons with peers are so salient (Henderson & Hennig, 1979). The influence of failure experiences on the learning of helplessness has been documented in a large number of studies with animal (e.g., Abramson, Seligman, & Teasdale, 1978) and human (e.g., Wortman,

Panciera, Shusterman, & Hibscher, 1976) subjects. In those studies that hold the clearest implications for children with exceptional needs, and more especially for those from culturally diverse backgrounds, the uncontrollable, aversive events that have led to perceptions of inability have involved the manipulation of feedback that lead subjects to believe they have failed problems that measure important human abilities (Roth & Kubal, 1975).

Effects of Learned Helplessness

In a series of studies, Dweck and her associates (Diner & Dweck, 1978; Dweck, 1975; Dweck & Busch, 1976; Dweck & Reppucci, 1973) found that children who have learned to feel helpless when confronted with difficult problems tend to attribute their failure to inability, while their nonhelpless peers often display improved performance following failure. Their improvement may be attributed to increased effort.

Helpless children are likely to see aversive situations as insurmountable and thus fail to display effort on subsequent tasks of the same sort. They are less likely to be willing to initiate a task or persist at it than are individuals who perceive their own effort as an important cause of success or failure outcomes. This is an important point, since there is evidence that differential instructional behaviors of teachers may be more associated with teacher judgments of pupil motivation to do school work than with achievement expectations (Luce & Hoge, 1978). This finding is particularly relevant in association with data showing that the behavior of teachers is markedly influenced by aspects of functional adaptation such as attending and nonattending behavior of students. Together these strands of evidence suggest that if helpless children respond to failure by declining to expend effort on subsequent tasks, teachers may react with negative expectations. Consequently, their interactions may be directed toward behavioral control rather than skill and content instruction.

Thomas (1979) has drawn attention to the striking parallels between the learned helplessness pattern and the characteristics of children classified as learning disabled. While the learning disabilities concept designates a diverse array of problems, Thomas noted that a common characteristic of children to whom this label is applied is that they are often convinced that they cannot learn. Consequently, a good deal of teaching is aimed at getting them to expend sufficient effort to achieve success (Thomas, 1979). The stronger a child's history of failure is, the more likelihood there is of self attributions of inability, and the likelihood of effortful, attentive behavior is concomitantly reduced. It seems that the nature of some schools in the United States almost predestines certain children to experience repeated failure, beginning with their earliest classroom experience. Since the socialization experience of culturally diverse children may not be highly congruent with the curricular and behavioral expectations of the middle class oriented school, a disproportionate number of them are at risk of falling into this group.

Failure, linked to perceptions of personal inability, may be coupled with negative affect (Ames, Ames & Felker, 1977). Failure may be experienced as a painful, punishing event, and the nature of responses to aversive stimuli are well documented. One response is escape or avoidance. Another is counter aggression (Henderson & Bergan, 1976). In the school context, either may be interpreted as alienation. Aversive failure experiences often produce anxiety, and a substantial body of research has documented the inverse relationship between anxiety and student ability to profit from instruction in school. Anxiety is linked to a range of academic indicators, including academic achievement and dropout rates (Tobias, 1979).

FACILITATING ENVIRONMENTS AND THERAPEUTIC APPROACHES

A number of instructional characteristics appear to facilitate perceptions of internal control and efficacy, while other procedures have been effective in increasing children's effort attributions. When children perceive a role in determining their own activities, they appear more likely to accept personal responsibility for success or failure than children in classrooms where no such opportunity to participate in the setting of objectives is provided (Arlin & Whitley, 1978; Wang & Stiles, 1976). It has also been demonstrated that the effects of success and failure are mediated by the kinds of social situations in which they occur. Classrooms constitute one of the few social settings in which children are routinely subjected to public comparisons of performance, and social comparisons are especially salient in those classrooms that employ competitive goal structures (Ames, Ames, & Felker, 1977; Henderson & Hennig, 1979). Failure is less likely to result in self depreciation in classrooms that employ a cooperative goal structure than in those characterized by norm referenced competition (Ames, Ames, & Felker, 1977).

A variety of therapeutic procedures have proved effective in changing dysfunctional attributions of cause (Henderson, in press). Since repeated failure experiences are implicated in the development of maladaptive attributions, it may seem logical that the way to change attributions from perceptions of inability to those of insufficient effort would be to provide generous portions of success. This appears not to be the case. Dweck

(1975) found that a success-only intervention did not improve the ability of helpless children to sustain effort following a failure experience. In fact, after a success-only intervention, many children showed a subsequent increase in sensitivity to failure. Children who were given a program of cognitively oriented attribution retaining displayed subsequent increases in effort attributions and improved adaptation to failure.

Both environmental control programs and self regulation programs have been found effective in changing socially and academically maladaptive classroom behavior. However, the effectiveness of a given procedure seems to interact with children's perceptions of causation. Bugenthal, Whalen, and Henker (1978) have recommended beginning with therapy that is in line with the child's perceptions of causation and moving toward procedures that provide greater self control through the application of self regulation strategies.

CONCLUSIONS AND IMPLICATIONS

Culturally diverse children are at risk of entering school with behaviors that differ from the cognitive and social norms governing the expectations of teachers who have been socialized into the school culture. These differences appear to play an important role in the reciprocal relationships among the child's capabilities, his or her actual behaviors, the teacher's expectancies, and the teacher's responses to the child. Differences in children's ability to adapt to school norms appear closely related to the level of formal education their own mothers have attained (Laosa, in press). Behaviors such as attentiveness and persistence at the kinds of tasks teachers consider important tend to influence the expectancies teachers hold, and these expectations, in turn, often influence the manner in which they interact with children.

Children whose behavior is discrepant from the norms of the school culture are likely to experience repeated failure. If, as a result, they develop feelings of helplessness in the school setting, they may well exert less and less effort, which in turn leads to more failure. An important social need of these children is to experience a feeling of personal efficacy. While it has been suggested that patterns of failure among culturally diverse children might be eliminated if the school would build systematically on abilities acquired by children in their home environments, it has proved more difficult than anticipated to put this suggestion into practice (Gallimore & Au, 1979).

One thing that can be done is to help teachers become aware of their own expectancies and variations in their instructional interactions with different children. Research on learned helplessness also suggests that it may help to structure classroom social environments in less competitive ways than has been traditional. In addition, children may be helped to gain a greater sense of efficacy if they are taught to set some of their own goals and to employ self regulation procedures. But therapeutic procedures based on experimental demonstrations are doomed to fall short if they are tagged on as remedial procedures in isolation from the on-going activities of a classroom. To do so would only provide an illusion of personal control and set children up for additional failure.

Bilingual and multicultural programs that enable children to experience cultural and linguistic pride certainly have an important role to play in meeting the social and emotional needs of children from diverse backgrounds (Gobson, 1978; Goebes & Shore, 1978), but they cannot fully accomplish their purposes unless children are helped to experience genuine feelings of personal and social competence within the total school setting. Existing research provides only indirect evidence relative to how reciprocal influences in classrooms might be turned to a better advantage for culturally diverse children. More specific research addressed to these dynamics is urgently needed.

REFERENCES

Abramson, N. L., Seligman, M. E. P., & Teasdale, J. D. Learned helplessness in humans: Critique and reformulation. *Journal of Abnormal Psychology,* 1978, *87,* 49–74.

Ames, C., Ames, R., & Felker, D. W. Effects of competitive reward structure and valence of outcome on children's achievement attributions. *Journal of Educational Psychology,* 1977, *69,* 1–8.

Anderson, S. B., & Messick, S. Social competence in young children. *Developmental Psychology,* 1974, *10,* 282–293.

Arlin, M., & Whitley, T. W. Perceptions of self-managed learning opportunities and academic locus of control: A causal interpretation. *Journal of Educational Psychology,* 1978, *70,* 988–992.

Brophy, J. E., & Good, T. *Teacher-student relationships: Causes and consequences.* New York: Holt, Rinehart & Winston, 1974.

Bugenthal, D., Whalen, C. K., & Henker. Causal attributions of hyperactive children and motivational assumptions of two behavior change approaches: Evidence for an interactionist position. *Child Development,* 1977, *48,* 874–884.

Chan, K. S., & Rueda, R. Poverty and culture in education: Separate but equal. *Exceptional Children,* 1979, *45,* 422–428.

Diner, C. I., & Dweck, C. S. An analysis of learned helplessness: Continuous changes in performance, strategy, and achievement conditions following failure. *Journal of Personality and Social Psychology,* 1978, *36,* 451–462.

Dweck, C. S. The role of expectations and attributions in the alleviation of learned helplessness. *Journal of Personality and Social Psychology,* 1975, *31,* 674–685.

Dweck, C. S., & Bush, E. S. Sex differences in learned helplessness: I. Differential debilitation with peer and adult evaluators. *Developmental Psychology,* 1976, *12,* 147–156.

Dweck, C. S., & Reppucci, N. D. Learned helplessness and reinforcement responsibility in children. *Journal of Personality and Social Psychology,* 1973, *25,* 109–116.

English, R. Beyond pathology: Research and theoretical perspectives on black families. In L. E. Gary (Ed.), *Social research and the black community: Selected issues and priorities.* Washington DC: Institute for Urban Affairs and Research, Howard University, 1974.

Evans-Pritchard, E. E. *Social Anthropology.* Glencoe IL: The Free Press, 1951.

Farris, B. E., & Glenn, N. D. Fatalism and familism among Anglos and Mexican Americans in San Antonio. *Sociology and Social Research,* 1976, *60,* 393–402.

Foster, G., & Ysseldyke, J. Expectancy and halo effects as a result of artificially induced teacher bias. *Contemporary Educational Psychology,* 1976, *1,* 37–45.

Gallimore, R., & Au, H. The competence/incompetence paradox in the education of minority culture children. *The Quarterly Newsletter of the Laboratory of Comparative Human Cognition,* 1979, *1,* 32–37.

Gibson, G. An approach to identification and prevention of developmental difficulties among Mexican-American children. *American Journal of Orthopsychiatry,* 1978, *48,* 96–113.

Goebes, D. D., & Shore, M. F. Some effects of bicultural and monocultural school environments on personality development. *American Journal of Orthopsychiatry,* 1978, *48,* 398–407.

Good, T. L., & Brophy, J. E. Changing teacher and student behavior: An empirical investigation. *Journal of Educational Psychology,* 1974, *66,* 390–405.

Gray-Little, B., & Applebaum, M. I. Instrumentality effects in the assessment of racial differences in self-esteem. *Journal of Personality and Social Psychology,* 1979, *37,* 1221–1229.

Hawkes, G. R., & Taylor, M. Power structure in Mexican and Mexican-American farm labor families. *Journal of Marriage and the Family,* 1975, *37,* 807–811.

Heider, F. *The psychology of interpersonal relations.* New York: Wiley, 1958.

Heller, C. S. *Mexican-American youth: Forgotten youth at the crossroads.* New York: Random House, 1966.

Henderson, R. W. Personal and social causation in the school context. In J. Worell (Ed.), *Developmental psychology for education.* New York: Academic Press, in press.

Henderson, R. W., & Bergan, J. R. *The cultural context of childhood.* Columbus OH: Charles E. Merrill, 1976.

Henderson, R. W., & Hennig, H. Relationships among cooperation-competition and locus of control in academic situations among children in traditional and open classrooms. *Contemporary Educational Psychology,* 1979, *4,* 121–131.

Hoge, R. D., & Luce, S. Predicting academic achievement from classroom behavior. *Review of Educational Research,* 1979, *49,* 479–496.

Kagan, S. & Buriel, R. Field dependence-independence and Mexican-American culture and education. In J. L. Martinez (Ed.), *Chicano psychology.* New York: Academic Press, 1977.

Knight, G. P., Kagan, S., Nelson, W., & Gumbiner, J. Acculturation of second and third generation Mexican-American children. Field independence, locus of control, self-esteem, and school achievement. *Journal of Cross-Cultural Psychology,* 1978, *9,* 87–98.

Kohm, M., & Rosman, B. L. A social competence scale and symptom checklist for the preschool child. Factor dimensions, their cross-instrument generality, and longitudinal perspectives. *Developmental Psychology,* 1972, *6,* 430–444.

Kroeber, A. L., & Kluckhohn, C. *Culture: A critical review of concepts and definitions.* New York: Vintage Books, 1952.

Laosa, L. M. Inequality in the classroom: Observational research on teacher-student interactions. *Aztlan International Journal of Chicano Studies Research,* 1977, *8,* 51–67.

Laosa, L. M. Maternal behavior: Sociocultural diversity in modes of family interaction. In R. W. Henderson (Ed.), *Parent-child interaction: Theory, research and prospect.* New York: Academic Press, in press.

Laosa, L. M. Social competence in childhood: Toward a developmental, socioculturally relativistic paradigm. In M. W. Kent & J. E Rolf (Eds.), *Primary Prevention of Psychopathology* (Vol. III). Hanover NH: University Press of New England, 1979.

Lefcourt, H. M. *Locus of control: Current trends in theory and research*. Hillsdale NJ: Lawrence Erlbaum Associates, 1976.

Linton, R. *The study of man*. New York: Appleton-Century-Crofts, 1936.

Luce, S. R., & Hoge, R. D. Relations among teacher rankings, pupil-teacher interactions, and academic achievement: A test of the teacher expectancy hypothesis. *American Educational Research Journal*, 1978, *15*, 489–500.

Madsen, W. *The Mexican-American of South Texas*. New York: Holt, Rinehart & Winston, 1964.

Monson, L. B., Greenspan, S., & Simeonsson, R. J. Correlates of social competence in retarded children. *American Journal of Mental Deficiency*, 1979, *83*, 627–630.

Moynihan, D. P. *The Negro family: The case for national action*. Washington DC: US Department of Labor, March, 1967.

Paz, O. *The labyrinth of solitude: Life and thought in Mexico*. New York: Grove Press, 1961.

Radcliffe-Browne, A. R. *A natural science of society*. Glencoe IL: The Free Press, 1957.

Richardson, J. G. The case of special education and minority misclassification in California. *Educational Research Quarterly*, 1979, *4*, 25–40.

Roth, S. & Kubal, L. The effects of noncontingent reinforcement on tasks of differing importance: Facilitation and learned helplessness effects. *Journal of Personality and Social Psychology*, 1975, *32*, 680–691.

Rotter, J. B. Generalized expectancies for internal versus external control of reinforcement. *Psychological Monographs*, 1966, *80*, (1, whole No. 609).

Thomas, A. Learned helplessness and expectancy factors: Implications for research in learning disabilities. *Review of Educational Research*. 1979, *49*, 220–221.

Tobias, S. Anxiety research in educational psychology. *Journal of Educational Psychology*, 1979, *71*, 573–582.

Wang, M. C., & Stiles, B. An investigation of children's concept of self-responsibility for school learning. *American Educational Research Journal*, 1976, *13*, 159–179.

Weiner, B. A theory of motivation for some classroom experiences. *Journal of Educational Psychology*, 1979, *71*, 3–25.

Wortman, C. B., Panciera, L., Shusterman, L., & Hibscher, J. Attributions of causality and reactions to uncontrollable outcomes. *Journal of Experimental Social Psychology*, 1976, *12*, 327–345.

Zigler, E., & Trickett, P. K. IQ, social competence, and evaluation of early childhood intervention programs. *American Psychologist*, 1978, *33*, 789–798.

Communicating with Parents of Culturally Diverse Exceptional Children

by Robert L. Marion

Working with parents of culturally diverse exceptional children should be considered an exacting challenge to teachers and educators in this decade. The adoption of such an attitude by professionals does not negate or overly subscribe to the problems that might arise between parents and educators with conflicting ideologies, values, and feelings. Rather, such a view recognizes that relationships between parents of culturally diverse handicapped and gifted children and professionals have been drastically altered by recent court decisions and legislative enactments. These pronouncements have produced significant attitudinal changes among the affected groups.

Most of the changes brought about through the courts or by legislation have been viewed as positive by parents who had previously been identified as disadvantaged, disenfranchised, or deprived. There have been several reasons for this response from culturally different parents. The *Mills* v. *the Board of Education* (1972) decision spoke to the issue of tracking. It forbade the District of Columbia schools to use a system of placement that resulted in the assignment of disproportionate numbers of minority students to the general or lowest curriculum track in the schools. The *Pennsylvania Association of Retarded Citizens (PARC)* v. *Pennsylvania* (1971) case was a significant victory for handicapped students and parents. It established the right of every mentally retarded child to have an opportunity for a free and appropriate public school education. The Education for All Handicapped Children Act of 1975 (Public Law 94-142) provided several guarantees to parents and clarified their roles as co-equal partners in the educational process. Protections that were of particular importance to parents of culturally diverse children were rights relating to due process, nondiscriminatory testing, and least restrictive environments.

To understand the significance that such parents attached to these developments, the similarities and differences in the educational process for culturally diverse gifted and handicapped children in the schools must be reviewed. The similarities can be summarized from the following viewpoints. First, parents of handicapped and gifted children should be considered parents of exceptional children. This statement can be interpreted within the framework that both categories of children have special educational, social, and personal needs (Cruickshank, 1975; Hoyt, 1976; Marland, 1972; Sato, 1974). Second, formal assessment has played a role in the assignment of numerous children to these divergent categories of exceptional children. This has been equally true for minority children and for nonminority children in society. Third, teacher perceptions have been a vital part of the total process of identifying gifted and handicapped students. Prior to Public Law 94-142, teachers were frequently the primary and even sole identifiers of handicapped children (Dunn, 1968; Hurley, 1969).

Some differences between the two categories of gifted and handicapped should be underscored, however. First, although both subsets are considered exceptional, giftedness has the connotation of excellence, of wisdom, of power. Handicapping conditions have the connotation of weakness, subnormality, and ugliness (Griffin, 1979). Second, assessment as utilized by the schools has played a far greater role in assigning culturally diverse populations to classrooms for mentally retarded children than to classes for the gifted (Dunn, 1968; Jones, 1972; Marion, 1979). Third, teacher nomination as a selection tool in the identification process has not been very successful in recognizing giftedness among culturally diverse children (Pegnato & Birch, 1959). It has been used with more accuracy in diagnosing culturally different pupils who are handicapped (Dunn, 1968; Hobbs, 1975; Jones, 1972).

REACTIONS OF PARENTS

The reactions of parents to these similarities and differences in the schooling process have led to a markedly different relationship between professionals and parents of culturally diverse gifted and handicapped students in contrast to their nonminority counterparts. The reactions of parents of culturally different children in both categories can probably be described differently from the way in which most of the literature to date has depicted them. Descriptions of the reactions of parents to the birth of their handicapped child include these terms: shock, disbelief, grief, mourning. A frantic search for a cause and a cure often accompanies these defense mechanisms. Many parents have been helped by professionals and other parents to accept the handicap of their child.

These reactions can be traced directly to studies of Anglo American parents. Much of the data was obtained from observing, examining, and reporting on the activities of nonminority parents. Not as much evidence on the same subject has been accumulated and documented with culturally diverse parents. One 3 year study (Marion & McCaslin, 1979) has served to substantiate the fact that many parents of culturally diverse handicapped children are not consumed with the same strong feelings as those that overwhelm nonminority parents. Luderus (1977) also supported the position that culturally different parents do not fit the stereotype generally ascribed to parents of handicapped children. Frequently, parents of culturally diverse handicapped children have not expressed shock, disbelief, sorrow, and some of the other associated feelings of guilt and depression. On the contrary, prior to Public Law 94-142, feelings of protection and acceptance of the handicapped child was the more typical emotion (Marion & McCaslin, 1979). This was especially true of Mexican-American and Black families, both of whom had extended family networks (Billingsley, 1968; Hill, 1972). Much of the research during this period did not stress the strengths of minority and culturally diverse families and tended to ascribe pathologicial conditions to atypical family structures (Minuchin, 1967; Myrdal, 1944). Many researchers also ignored the role of religion and the feelings of acceptance and security engendered by its place of prominence in culturally diverse families (Billingsley, 1968; Cole, 1967; Hill, 1972).

The burden of having a handicapped child in the family was probably most strongly fixed in the minds of culturally diverse parents when their child entered school (Barsch, 1969). Faced with large numbers of culturally different children in urban areas, regular school systems showed their inability to accommodate these children by assigning increasing numbers of them to special education classes (Dunn, 1968; Hobbs, 1975; Jones, 1972). Special education aided in this movement by the reciprocal acceptance of these children into classes for the mentally retarded (Hurley, 1969; Hurley, 1971). Therefore, in the 1970's great numbers of culturally diverse children grew up in the special education system and, as adolescents, have become products of a self fulfilling prophecy (Larsen, 1975).

The greatest reaction expressed by parents of culturally diverse handicapped children has been one of anger and dismay at the policy of overinclusion of their children in classes for the mentally retarded and emotionally disturbed. This policy, as practiced by the schools, has permeated the thinking of culturally diverse families to such an extent that they have become desperate and confused. The anger displayed by these parents has been a reaction against an educational system that they feel has promoted these two categories as the only appropriate depositories for their children (Hurley, 1971; Marion, 1979).

Parents of culturally diverse gifted students have not reacted to a policy of inclusion but rather to school practices of exclusion. Although gifted children are considered exceptional children, parents of culturally diverse gifted students have been less than optimistic about the chances that their children will gain entry into programs for talented students (Marion, in press). Pessimistic reactions to the heavy reliance by schools upon IQ tests as the major discerner of giftedness in students is common. Only when a marriage between "nature" and "nurture" theories is effected are parents of culturally diverse gifted children given to hope that their children might be included in these programs.

Many of the frustrations of parents of culturally diverse gifted populations have also revolved around the condition of schooling for adolescents. Parents are concerned that many culturally diverse problem adolescents of today were yesterday's gifted and talented children (Shaw, 1978). As younger children they might have been described as:

1. Members of large, financially insecure, and *a priori* love families.
2. Exhibiting inappropriate social behavior.
3. Popular with their classmates and possessing more social insight than their peers.

Parents are fearful that a goodly number of adolescents who demonstrated these tendencies to teachers were mislabeled *emotionally disturbed, socially maladjusted,* or *mentally retarded* on the strength of atypical family characteristics or culturally different mannerisms.

CONCERNS OF PARENTS

Many of the concerns of parents of culturally diverse gifted and handicapped children are creations of the negative image that education has projected. Consequently, many of the difficulties in the communication process can be traced directly to this undesirable image. For instance, special education has clung tenaciously to the view that the perfect family corresponds to an average US Census family, comprised of two parents and two children. Most culturally diverse families, especially the poor, exceed this family size, which immediately implies that they are atypical. Such an image strains the traditional concept of giftedness, when its presence is acknowledged solely in an only child or in the eldest of two children (Barbe, 1965). Likewise, parents of culturally different handicapped children have been made to feel guilty about their large families.

Testing

Perhaps the concern that has caused most friction to occur between schools and culturally diverse populations with gifted and handicapped children has been the issue of testing. This issue has occupied the thinking of culturally diverse groups for a long time (Gay & Abraham, 1974; Oakland, 1974). Reasons for this preoccupation with the testing issue have been well documented through the courts (*Diana* v. *State Board of Education,* 1973; *Larry P.* v. *Riles,* 1972). The concern of parents of handicapped children has centered upon the use of tests to disproportionately assign their children to classes for the mentally retarded or the emotionally disturbed (Children's Defense Fund, 1974; Hurley, 1971). Parents of culturally diverse handicapped children have complained that prior to Public Law 94-142 their opinions were not solicited and they did not have any input into the placement of their children (Children's Defense Fund, 1975; Hickerson, 1966; Southern Regional Council, 1974).

With regard to culturally diverse gifted children, the uneasy truce between "nature" and "nurture" opponents has failed to quiet the differences of opinion concerning the potential for giftedness among this group. Although the definition of giftedness has been broadened, schools continue to support the idea that intelligence is measured by an IQ obtained through testing (Mercer, 1973).

Identification

A final concern that has troubled parents of culturally diverse gifted and handicapped children has been the question of teacher identification. This issue has emerged because many studies report on the inability of teachers to recognize giftedness among culturally different children (Malone, 1975; Pegnato & Birch, 1959). Traditional indicators upon which observations are based are usually middle class values, family stereotypes, and teacher expectations about conformist pupil behavior (Larsen, 1975; McCandless, 1967). In the eyes of many teachers, culturally diverse gifted populations fail to measure up to these indicators (Marion, 1979). On the other hand, many culturally diverse handicapped children are in fact identified and placed into special education (Prillman, 1975).

COMMUNICATING WITH PARENTS

Parents of culturally diverse gifted and handicapped students have exhibited a number of common needs. When these needs have been met, the views of culturally diverse parents have generally been changed to a more positive outlook and communication has been facilitated. Professionals who are attempting to work with these parents should have an understanding of these needs to effectively expand their roles in the communication process.

Need for Information

The need for information constitutes one of the primary requests from parents of culturally diverse gifted and handicapped children. In communicating with parents of handicapped children, much of this need can be satisfied through regularly scheduled meetings and conferences and planning sessions for the individualized education program (IEP). Many educators assume that their own familiarity with Public Law 94-142 is automatically bestowed upon the parents. Nothing is further from the truth. Some parents of culturally diverse handicapped children need to further understand the basic tenets of Public Law 94-142, including their rights and responsibilities. Educators working with parents should be certain that they:

1. Have a knowledge of the law itself and of corresponding regulations.
2. Have a thorough knowledge of their clients.
3. Can effect communication among staff members, between parents and the agencies which are to serve their child, and, in some cases, between staff and the client they are assisting.
4. Utilize appropriate times and settings for parent-teacher conferences.

Only well informed parents can be intelligent consumers of information. There should be agreement that parents and educators have one common denominator, their concern for the education and welfare of children.

Parents of gifted culturally diverse children have experienced many problems similar to those of their counterparts with handicapped children. They, too, have an information gap when qualitative and quantitative differences of giftedness are being discussed. Many parents have not been made aware of the broadened definition of gifted children as those individuals who excel consistently or show the potential for excelling consistently in any human endeavor—academic, creative, kinesthetic (performance skills), or psychosocial (relational and leadership skills). Parents must exchange information to be assured that the broadened definition will not perpetuate segregation within gifted education, that is, nonminority children being placed in all academically gifted classes and culturally diverse pupils going into what would be considered ''talented only'' sections.

Educators who are attempting to exchange information with parents of culturally diverse students should be prepared to engage in time consuming tasks. Sometimes the parents' lack of knowledge can actually be caused by educators who tend to hold back information under the assumption that culturally different parents are not sophisticated enough to grasp the material. Rather than assume this stance, professionals should be putting into effect the following guidelines:

1. Send messages home in language parents understand.
2. Work with children to prevent previous negative experiences from having a lasting impression.
3. Respect the parents enough to listen for messages being returned.

Communicating in a clear, concise manner implies that professionals and parents exchange information in layman's terms. Educators should have a sensitivity to Ebonics (Black dialectical differences) and bilingualism and not be offended by different syntaxes or speech patterns used by some culturally diverse populations. On the receiving end, educators should be understanding of the fact that some parents of culturally different children have not profited from all the established communication vehicles used by nonminority parents. Many parents of culturally diverse children have not actively gathered information by affiliating with professional organizations (Marion, 1979; Roos, 1976). Those individuals lacking the ability to handle the sophisticated reading level of much of today's literature have not been able to familiarize themselves with written material. Many do not belong to social cliques that obtain and exchange information on an impromptu basis.

In facing these situations educators must have an accepting attitude. When parents and professionals continue to exchange information, the apathetic and confused parent can be replaced by the parent who wants to know:

1. Whether or not programs for all ages exist.
2. How the schools go about identifying exceptional children.
3. About procedures for evaluating children.
4. How children are placed in programs.
5. About due process.
6. Who their allies are. (U.S. Department of Health, Education & Welfare, 1976a, p. 4)

Educators will have to listen empathetically and realize that feelings of parents can change from trust to skepticism and/or curiosity. They may be critical of school policies and procedures. Teachers should realize that this reaction is normal and that parents may be hostile and desperate as they attempt to sort out facts from their fundamental beliefs about education.

Professionals who are attempting to work and communicate with parents are facing an important task (Rogers, 1961). They should be prepared to listen and be ready to join forces with parents concerning their rights and responsibilities. In essence, professionals should adopt the role of advocate with parents of culturally diverse children. Educators must report factual information in an objective fashion. By responding in this manner they can establish mutual positions of trust and respect.

Need to Belong

Another basic need of parents of culturally diverse gifted and handicapped children has been the need to belong. The same need applies to both categories in spite of obvious differences in the students. Parents with culturally different gifted and handicapped children are not well represented in the membership of parent organizations of either category. Some parent groups are unwilling to recruit culturally diverse populations into their organizations. Often an unstable family financial condition has contributed to the situation. Families struggling to meet basic survival needs may be unwilling to join dues paying associations. Moreover, if they have been experiencing basic survival needs, parents of culturally different children can be expected to be reluctant to associate with a membership comprised of people who have different socioeconomic and cultural backgrounds and interests.

The outcome of this nonalliance has been a feeling of isolation on the part of parents with culturally different children. These parents have often felt as if they were either unwanted visitors or undesirables. All too often the feeling of isolation has been brought on by an unfair appraisal of the family structure. It has not been easy for these parents to sit in on meetings where discussions about family characteristics and relationships are emphasizing issues foreign to their interests. Those who remain are often seen but not heard (Marion, 1979).

Schools have not successfully met the challenge of helping parents overcome their feelings of isolation and loneliness, either. They have practiced a policy of exclusion against the culturally different (Cohen, 1970). Language, speech, and racial differences have stamped certain groups of children as outsiders. Student pushouts, dropouts, and suspensions have characterized the schools' reactions to people who vary from the nonminority population (Southern Regional Council, 1974).

Nevertheless, the major responsibility for alleviating parental feelings of indifference and isolation remains with schools and teachers. They have been ranked second only to the family in importance in the lives of children (Hobbs, 1975). Parents can be helped to shed the feelings of loneliness if professionals will not label them with such stereotypes as "rejecting," "hostile," or "demanding." Educators and other professionals should:

1. Assure parents that they should not feel guilty about their child's exceptionality or problem.
2. Accept the parents' feelings without labeling them.
3. Accept parents as people—not a category.
4. Help parents to see the positives in the future.
5. Respect the need for parents . . . to value their lives highly.
6. Recognize . . . what a big job it is to raise an exceptional child and help parents to find . . . the range of programs, services, and financial resources needed to make it possible for parents to do the job with dignity. (U.S. Department of Health, Education, & Welfare, 1976b, p. 2)

Teachers and other professionals will have to become advocates for the inclusion of parents of culturally different children into organizations mainly frequented by nonminority parents. Culturally different parents should be encouraged to join parent organizations and present minority points of view. Educators will have to collaborate with parents to give them coping skills for joining and maintaining membership in such groups. Recruitment efforts might be strengthened with the addition of dues waivers for parents experiencing financial difficulties. Social isolation of culturally diverse parents will be reduced when their group numbers increase to the point where the majority membership acknowledges their presence.

Using these guidelines, teachers and other professionals will be assisting parents of culturally diverse gifted and handicapped children not only to combat feelings of isolation but also to achieve a sense of belonging.

Need for Positive Self Esteem

Maslow (1962) established the need for high self esteem as a fundamental issue in the hierarchy of needs. Parents of culturally diverse handicapped children have not experienced much enhancement of their self esteem as the schools have steadily increased the numbers of their children in classes for the mentally retarded or the emotionally disturbed. Their counterparts with gifted children have also suffered from a lack of self esteem. It has been pointed out to them that their children have consistently fallen short of measures of giftedness as determined by IQ tests. For both groups of parents it has been implied that family structures, economic class, and heredity all work to their detriment when they are compared to their majority counterparts (Jensen, 1969; Minuchin, 1967).

Parents in culturally diverse populations have a need to be understood. They are asking that professionals recognize their feelings and be responsive to them. Parents who have raised children in a cooperative atmosphere cannot be blamed for their alarm when this quality is not valued as highly as initiative in the school environment (Billingsley, 1968; Hill, 1972). Furthermore, Americans tend to pride themselves on "fighting against the odds and not giving up." Those persons who have not continually subscribed to this notion have often been accused of "sluffing off." Stouteartedness and perseverance are expected of parents no matter what type of stress they may be confronting (Hudson, 1976). Parental reactions to these expectations have sometimes resulted in anger and loss of self esteem.

Professionals working with minority parents should capitalize on emotion to rebuild the self esteem of parents. Anger can be used to mobilize the parents into action. Parents should be urged to:

1. Know the law.
2. Work with other parents.
3. Work with professionals.
4. Use their right to speak.
5. Stop pleading; education is a right.
6. Learn how to take part in planning conferences.
7. Not compromise and insist on full evaluation and clear goals.
8. Be an active citizen. (U.S. Department of Health, Education, & Welfare, 1976b, p. 2)

Without question, educators and other professionals will have to continue their advocacy roles to assist parents of culturally diverse gifted and handicapped children in pursuing the prescribed actions. Parents are typically unwilling to undertake these assignments without the help of a committed, responsible professional.

However, these actions cannot be accomplished solely through teacher advocacy. The advocacy role for teachers will best be combined with an ombudsman approach. Educators are in a position to mediate any intense feelings that parents may have as they experience the stresses of rearing and educating their culturally different gifted and handicapped children. In these difficult times in the lives of parents, many will be heard saying that they do not need trials to build character (Hudson, 1976). Teachers should be prepared to deal with that attitude. They should seek to strengthen the self concept of parents by aligning themselves with the parents. Teachers place themselves in an understanding position by acknowledging frustrations and anger. Working from this stance, professionals can resolve some of the temporary affective blocks that hinder communication. They can diminish the chance that they will be perceived as experts or authority figures. If parents are led to feel that they lack the qualifications necessary to meet the needs of their child, it can only serve to intimidate them. As a result, the parents' self concept is further diminished and any additional attempts at communication are thwarted. Educators who are seeking to work effectively with parents of culturally diverse gifted and handicapped children have recognized that this outcome is in direct opposition to the intended goal of facilitating communication.

Instead, teachers should continually seek to mobilize the energy of parents toward productive ends. Professionals should help parents find satisfaction in learning what can be done for their child and working actively for the child's maximum potential development. As a result, the gains that parents see in their children will become a source of continued motivation. Using this approach, educators can increase the confidence of parents. Convincing parents to work for better public understanding of their children, to improve facilities and increase funding, will result in their increased self esteem.

CONCLUSION

Communicating with parents of culturally diverse gifted and handicapped children is a time consuming task. For these parents the realization that their children will be thought of as "special" students can be expected to produce varied reactions. Professionals who work with parents of culturally different students should be prepared to meet their needs for belonging, self esteem, and information. Also, educators must be guided by an appreciation of dialectical deviations, a respect for cultural differences, and faith in the concept of individualized instruction. Professionals must be prepared to provide help at the cognitive and affective levels as they work with parents who are traditionally outside the mainstream of American education. Successfully meeting these needs and expectations will help educators move toward the goal of improving communication between professionals and parents of culturally diverse gifted and handicapped children.

REFERENCES

Barbe, W. B. A study of the family background of the gifted. In W. B. Barbe (Ed.), *Psychology and education of the gifted*. New York: Appleton-Century-Crofts, 1965.

Barsch, R. *The parent-teacher partnership*. Arlington VA: The Council for Exceptional Children, 1969.

Billingsley, A. *Black families in White America*. Englewood Cliffs NJ: Prentice-Hall, 1968.

Children's Defense Fund. *Children out of school in America*. Cambridge MA: Author, 1974.

Children's Defense Fund. *School suspensions: Are they helping children?* Cambridge MA: Author, 1975.

Cohen, D. Immigrants and the schools. *Review of Educational Research*, 1970, *40* (1), 13–15.

Cole, R. *Children of crisis*. Boston: Little, Brown, & Co., 1967.

Cruickshank, W. W. *Psychology of exceptional children and youth*. Englewood Cliffs NJ: Prentice-Hall, 1975.

Diana v. *State Board of Education*. Civil Action No. C-70, 37RFP (N.D. Cal. January 7, 1970 & June 18, 1973).

Dunn, L. M. Special education for the mildly retarded—Is much of it justifiable? *Exceptional Children*, 1968, *35*, 5–21.

Gay, G., & Abrahams, R. Does the pot melt, boil, or brew? Black children and assessment procedures. *Journal of School Psychology*, 1974, *11* (4), 330–340.

Griffin, H. *Attitudes, opinions and general information concerning cerebral palsy.* Unpublished doctoral dissertation, University of Texas, 1979.

Hickerson, N. *Education for alienation*. Englewood Cliffs NJ: Prentice-Hall, 1966.

Hill, R. *The strengths of Black families*. New York: Emerson Hall, 1972.

Hobbs, N. *The futures of children*. Nashville: Vanderbilt University Press, 1975.

Hoyt, K. *Career education for special populations*. Washington DC: U. S. Government Printing Office, 1976.

Hudson, K. Helping parents to help their handicapped child. In *Proceedings, the Institute for Deaf-Blind Studies*, Sacramento, 1976, 75–78.

Hurley, O. *Special education in the inner city: The social implications of placement*. Paper presented at the Conference on Placement of Children in Special Education Programs for the Mentally Retarded, President's Committee on Mental Retardation, Lake Arrowhead, March 7–10, 1971.

Hurley, R. *Poverty and mental retardation: A causal relationship*. New York: Vintage, 1969.

Jensen, A. How much can we boost I.Q. and scholastic achievement? *Harvard Educational Review*, 1969, *39*, 2.

Jones, R. *Black psychology*. New York: Harper & Row, 1972.

Larry P. v. *Riles*. Civil Action No. C-71-2270 343F, Supp. 1306 (N.D. Cal., 1972).

Larsen, S. The influence of teacher expectations on the school performance of handicapped children. *Focus on Exceptional Children*, 1975, *6*, 6–7.

Luderus, E. *Family environment characteristics of Mexican-American families of handicapped and non-handicapped preschool children.* Unpublished doctoral dissertation, University of Texas, 1977.

Malone, C., & Moonan, W. Behavioral identification of gifted children. *Gifted Child Quarterly, 19,* 301–306, 289.

Marion, R. L. Counseling parents of the disadvantaged or culturally different gifted. *The Roeper Review,* in press.

Marion, R. L. Minority parent involvement in the IEP process: A systematic model approach. *Focus on Exceptional Children,* 1979, *10,* 1–14.

Marion, R. L., & McCaslin, T. *Parent counseling of minority parents in a genetic setting.* Unpublished manuscript, University of Texas, 1979.

Marland, S. *Education of the gifted and talented: Report to the Congress of the United States by the U.S. Commissioner of Education.* Washington DC: U.S. Government Printing Office, 1972.

Maslow, A. *Toward a psychology of being.* Princeton: Van Nostrand, 1962.

McCandless, B. *Children behavior and development.* New York: Holt, Rinehart, & Winston, 1967.

Mercer, J. *Labeling the mentally retarded.* Berkeley: University of California Press, 1973.

Mills v. *Board of Education of the District of Columbia.* 348 F. Supp. 866 (D.D.C. 1972).

Minuchin, S., et al. *Families of the slums: An exploration of their structure and treatment.* New York: Basic Books, 1967.

Myrdal, G. *An American Dilemma.* New York: Harper, 1944.

Oakland, T. Assessing minority group children: Challenges for school psychologists. *Journal of School Psychology,* 1974, *4,* 294–303.

Pegnato, C. W., & Birch, J. W. Locating gifted children in junior high schools: A comparison of methods. *Exceptional Children,* 1959, *25,* 300–304.

Pennsylvania Association for Retarded Children (PARC) v. *Commonwealth of Pennsylvania,* 343F Supp. 279 (E.D. pa., 1972), Consent Agreements.

Prillman, D. *Virginia EMR study.* Bloomington IN: Phi Delta Kappa, 1975.

Rogers, C. R. *On becoming a person.* Boston: Houghton Mifflin, 1961.

Roos, P. Panel discussion. American Association of Mental Deficiency National Conference. Chicago IL, 1976.

Shaw, C. *Imaginative investigations: Development of a creative writing course for gifted Black adolescents.* Unpublished masters thesis, The University of Texas, 1978.

Southern Regional Council. *The pushout,* Atlanta GA: Author, 1974.

U.S. Department of Health, Education and Welfare, Office of Education, Bureau of Education for the Handicapped. Know your rights. *Closer Look,* Winter, 1976a, 3–5.

U.S. Department of Health, Education and Welfare, Office of Education, Bureau of Education for the Handicapped. Professionals: Are you listening. *Closer Look,* Winter 1976b, 2–4.

Career Opportunities for Culturally Diverse Handicapped Youth

by George W. Fair and Allen R. Sullivan

Critical and somewhat contradictory concerns have been expressed relative to the provision of career and vocational educational opportunities for culturally diverse youth (Wells, 1978). There is little research specifically addressing issues related to the provision of educational opportunities for culturally diverse youth with handicaps. This article first provides an overview of the employment situation for minority individuals and its implications for career and vocational education of culturally diverse handicapped youth. Second, the article delineates the enigma presented by being a member of a doubly stigmatized population, that is, culturally diverse handicapped youth. Attention is given to the barriers to effective educational and employment opportunities for this population. Finally, the article forecasts the prospects of career and vocational education and makes recommendations for future programing and research.

RACE, CULTURE, HANDICAPS: EMPLOYMENT

"Changes in Society Holding Black Youth in a Jobless Web" (Herbers, 1979), along with a series of four other articles, described the plight of the Black youth in reference to employment opportunities. In this article, Labor Secretary Ray Marshall indicated that unemployment among Black youths between the ages of 16 and 19 was as high as 38.3%. This is considered a conservative estimate by many. The unemployment picture for minority youth, particularly Blacks, is now roughly what it was for the entire nation during the Great Depression. Although racial discrimination in employment was made illegal by the Civil Rights Act of 1964, and although successive court decisions have upheld the right of equal access to jobs, job discrimination, while more subtle than before, still remains (Herbers, 1979).

Stereotypes exist in society that make securing employment extremely difficult for culturally diverse handicapped youth. Little professional attention has been paid to the interaction among race, gender and handicapping conditions, which, when combined, may identify the most discriminated class of people within our society. Paradoxically, these persons, when employed, may well be the most stable working force. An illustration of this point can be found in a survey conducted by the US Office of Vocational Rehabilitation (Halloran, 1978) on the experiences with handicapped employees of more than 100 large corporations. Of the corporations reporting, 66% said there were no differences between handicapped individuals and abled bodied individuals in productivity. Furthermore, 24% rated handicapped persons higher in productivity. Thus, 90% were perceived to be equal to or surpassing the productivity of nonhandicapped individuals. The study further indicated that 57% reported lower accident rates, 55% reported lower absenteeism rates, and 83% reported lower turnover rates for handicapped persons. Providing this information could go a long way in reducing the xenophobic response expressed or implied by potential employers, that is, the fear that employing handicapped individuals will present personnel problems for the company.

OVERVIEW OF VOCATIONAL TRAINING OPPORTUNITIES

For women and minorities, vocational education has been used to reinforce society's notion of their proper or realistic role in society. Halloran (1978) suggested that vocational institutions should focus their attention on the effects of handicapping conditions that can be remedied. He further pointed out that more than two-thirds of vocational education for the handicapped is not intended to prepare students to compete on the open labor market in a given skill, craft, or trade. Lee (1975) indicated that approximately 1.7% of students enrolled in vocational education programs are handicapped youth. Because of the criticism of traditional vocational education and because so few poor, minority, and handicapped youth were included, the Comprehensive Employment and Training Act (CETA) program was developed and included more than double the number of handicapped persons (4%) that were in traditional vocational education programs. Levitan and Taggart (1976) found that 40% of disabled adults are employed compared with 75% of the nondisabled population. Average weekly wages of employed disabled males are 22% lower than those of their nondisabled counterparts. In summary, these findings indicate that, to date, programs that have legislative, professional, and moral responsibility for providing meaningful training opportunities for handicapped individuals have been less than adequate. Thus, the very programs designed to address the needs of bypassed populations, victims of systematic discrimination and exclusion, perpetuate the identical practice and philosophy. One reason this practice continues may be fear or apprehension on the part of potential employers and trainers in terms of working with handicapped individuals. This concern was addressed by Wright (1960) in her classic book concerning physical disability. She indicated that "existing values, concepts, and factual information can go far in relieving suffering and aiding social and psychological rehabilitation, if only applied more genuinely'and generally in the ordinary affairs of life as well as among the many special enterprises that society as a whole needs to undertake" (p. 380).

The Comptroller General's 1974 report to Congress indicated that the federal government's priority of providing vocational opportunities for disadvantaged and handicapped students had not cascaded to the state and local level. The report further expressed concern about the small number of students receiving these services compared with the large number needing them. One of the dangers currently confronting the provisions for handicapped and culturally divese youth is the back to basics trend in education. The back to basics or back to the good old days phenomenon presents problems for populations who were denied equal opportunities in those "good old days." Those days were good for only some people. Valverde (1977) postulated that the back to basics trend is attempting to solve novel problems of education's advancement by simply reverting to former practices with their familiar frustrations.

BARRIERS TO ACHIEVEMENT

There are several specific barriers to the education and employment of handicapped individuals and their quest for educational equity and excellence:

1. *Architectural barriers* deprive mobility limited persons from access to the place of employment and instructional facilities.

2. *Ideological barriers* are imposed by limited vision or myopic response to the abilities of culturally diverse handicapped persons, therefore limiting the perception of what skills a student can master.

3. *Procedural barriers* are created by procedures that do not adequately search for, identify, counsel, and select culturally diverse handicapped students in the full continuum of vocational and career training opportunities.

4. *Substantive barriers* are imposed by limiting the scope and sequence of the curriculum. This occurs by focusing on a narrow band of vocational skills without taking into consideration an individual student's motivation, personal preference, and need to develop social competencies. These barriers are also reflected in the type of clusters offered in vocational programs that exclude areas such as retailing, technical, and scientific services and emphasize instead human service areas such as food preparation and delivery, housekeeping, and maintenance.

5. *Affective barriers* are personal in nature, and influence an individual's feelings about culturally diverse handicapped persons, engendering inappropriate sympathy or apathy, or fostering protective or rejecting behaviors, respectively.

THE CHALLENGE TO CHANGE

When specifically focusing on minority youth, the whole specter of racism enters the picture. The history of negative responses to minority and racial groups has been well documented. Any solutions to problems concerning this topic as it relates to handicapped youth would have to be blended into a systematic civil rights thrust. Many groups such as the Urban League, the Urban Coalition, and several Black fraternal and social groups have attempted to address the issues of motivation and effective educational programing for minority youth. These groups should be encouraged to add a component for handicapped youth.

As reported by Wells (1978), the US Office of Education conducted a study of the attitudes of more than 1,000 Black leaders, including vocational educators, and found a general lack of enthusiasm for vocational education programs as generally constituted. "The study concluded that Blacks believe formal vocational education programs 'limit the employment and leadership potential of the student more than some alternative types of job training programs' " (p. 46). The criticism could continue. For example, one major criterion for the selection of teachers in vocational programs is that they have had significant experience in the field. When this requirement is coupled with documented failures of the labor movement to affirmatively involve minority and racial groups into the mainstream of employment opportunities, there is a strong possibility that vocational teachers may lack experience and sensitivity in addressing issues that provide legitimate vocational opportunities for culturally diverse youth. The selection and hiring practices of schools reduce the possibility that culturally distinct students will have relevant vocational role models.

DIRECTIONS

Adelman and Phelps (1978) identified several program components that they believe are essential in developing a vocational program for handicapped youth. These same components are necessary for culturally diverse handicapped youth.

1. *Individualization* does not mean a student is taught in isolation, but it suggests that there may be special and unique needs for particular individuals.
2. *Student analysis* is an assessment of the strengths, interests, and skills that a student has including manual dexterity, work capacity, and motivation.
3. *Task analysis* is matching the student's skills to the specific occupational competencies he or she will be learning.
4. *Program analysis* is deciding whether general or specific training in an occupational cluster will be provided to the student.

In general, Adelman and Phelps indicated that the handicapped student should be given good faith opportunity to learn through the presentation of clearly thought out experiences.

Strategies for Success

In a paper entitled "Retaining Blacks in Science: An Effective Model," Young and Young (1979) identified strategies for enabling unprepared or disadvantaged students to succeed in technical college level programs. Many of these strategies are applicable to enabling culturally diverse handicapped individuals to succeed in technical career development programs. The following is an expansion of the suggestions by Young and Young (1979) that can be used in career and vocational education programs in which culturally diverse handicapped students are enrolled.

1. Begin Instruction of Students' Present Level. The first suggestion deals with the process of beginning instruction. Many programs in secondary schools make assumptions about the prerequisite skills that a student possesses upon entering the program. The recommendation is that the instructor take enough time to adequately assess each student in reference to these prerequisite skills and begin instruction based on this data. Reading and math grade level scores obtained by standardized testing are often used to convey the degree of competence in these areas, and instruction often begins based on this data. Such a procedure is not satisfactory for culturally diverse handicapped students. These judgments should be based on valid assessment activities that are nondiscriminatory in nature and that are employment and job related.

2. Utilize Mastery Learning Objectives. The second suggestion is related to the mastery learning concept. Many persons with stereotyped ideas immediately think of lowering standards when culturally diverse or handicapped persons are concerned. If there is a clear articulation of what the standards and objectives are, a lowering of standards is not necessary. The objectives should be clearly defined and alternative modes of instruction should be made available in order to meet these objectives. If appropriate and adequate opportunities are made available to culturally diverse handicapped students the lowering of standards need never be considered.

3. Accommodate Differences in Learning Styles. Most professionals in special education understand that students with learning problems may have different learning styles. This is obviously true for culturally diverse handicapped students as well. The important point to remember is that this group does not, within itself, have any homogenous learning style. The statements that attempt to attribute particular learning characteristics to certain minority groups are simply not valid.

4. Provide a Positive Psychological Climate. A positive psychological climate is one where a good rapport exists between students and teachers, and an expectation of success prevails. It is developed from mutual respect on the part of both students and teachers. Teachers need to have a pluralistic frame of reference which acknowledges that all people have something of value to offer and that cultural and linguistic differences are societal assets. Success experiences are also a part of a positive psychological climate. Such experiences are fostered by the adoption of appropriate expectations and provision of sufficient opportunities to succeed.

5. Enable Students to Build an Internal Sense of Responsibility. Enabling students to build a sense of personal responsibility means that students should be encouraged to feel that they have a degree of involvement in determining their own fate. Culturally diverse handicapped students need to realize that there exists a relationship between their behavior and what happens to them. As a culturally diverse handicapped person it is understandable and somewhat realistic to think that people will make prejudgments about one's ability and that certain opportunities will not become available. This type of orientation may be counterproductive to developing the degree of competence that is needed to be the master of one's own fate.

6. Provide a Well Articulated, Comprehensive, Cohesive Program Structure. Successful programs for culturally diverse handicapped students should be comprehensive and cohesive. Special education and vocational education instructors, counselors, and other helping professionals need to work together for the benefit of these students. Such cooperation should take the form of planning and organization that will be proactive and

participatory, therefore preventing problems from developing rather than being remedial and providing only temporary solutions to crises. Coordination has been lacking in many programs that require the contributions of a significant number of people, disciplines, and agencies. Without question, if culturally diverse handicapped children are to be meaningfully served in career and vocational education programs, cooperation and coordination must improve.

7. Provide Comprehensive Personnel Development. For success to occur a systematic and comprehensive staff development component should be added to career and vocational education programs. The majority of occupational education teachers state that they were not trained to work with special needs students. Their training should not be independent from the training of other staff members who are involved with handicapped youth. The special education staff should become more familiar with vocational assessment and programming. Sheppard (1966) and Schwartz (1967) stipulated that preservice and inservice training must provide teachers with many opportunities for solving problems related to adapting programs and practices for handicapped youth, clarifying their own values, and recognizing ambiguities and ambivalence in their own beliefs and in the beliefs of others.

8. Facilitate Career Planning. Career planning is an area where monumental efforts are needed for culturally diverse handicapped students. People think about potential occupations on the basis of preceptions that are often sketchy or inaccurate. This is particularly significant for culturally diverse handicapped students because of the lack of exposure they may have to occupations. The decisions that one makes based on incomplete information can affect an entire lifetime. It is difficult for most students and especially for culturally diverse handicapped students to obtain informal exposure to a variety of occupations because of the barriers and other conditions discussed earlier.

Appropriate career planning encompasses many activities. It should include early occupational experiences that permit individuals to expand their knowledge and increase their awareness of the range of occupational alternatives. Such planning should recognize the contributions that persons of specific cultural and ethnic backgrounds have made to society. Students must also be made aware that racism does exist in society and that it places additional demands on certain students.

In light of the fiscal considerations, workload, and training of present counselors, the one to one counseling model will not meet the needs of the culturally diverse handicapped student who should participate in such a program. The new model should be community based and include contributions by parents and other nonschool personnel. Advantages of such a model enable culturally diverse handicapped students to identify their own abilities, interests, and values. Occupational information should be combined with a personal evaluation. The individuals can then be helped to identify job market trends and characteristics and relate the characteristics and requirements of various occupations to their individual abilities, interests, and values. Pertinent occupational information should also allow the students to identify the sequence of activities that are required to enter a given occupation. In this way, appropriate career planning becomes an effective vehicle in providing more opportunities for culturally diverse handicapped students.

FUTURE

Particular trends and issues will merit critical attention in the next 10 years. It is evident that the schools will have the major responsibility for preparing culturally diverse handicapped youth with basic skills and work skills. The schools, although criticized by many persons, are still best prepared to accomplish this task. Innovative and dynamic school leadership that interfaces with all aspects of the community will be demanded to a greater extent than ever before. Alternative institutions have developed for those students for whom the school has not been effective. Cooperation between these institutions and the schools should be encouraged. Such institutions provide a healthy diversification of approaches and vary in their vocational focus, methods of delivery, institutional structure, and means of support. However, the schools will continue to be the greatest force in providing for the needs of culturally diverse handicapped students.

The focus of school programs for these young people needs to center on long term employability and job related skills. Special education, with its work-study programs, has not always focused on long term employment needs. Programs must be expanded to provide vocational training and job related skills before job placement is considered. Such programs must have adequate resources and equipment and provide for continuous job supervision and rewards for exemplary performance.

A coordinated governmental thrust is necessary to ensure that programs developed to focus on career and vocational needs have processes that include culturally diverse handicapped youth. Such programs should be strongly encouraged to incorporate successful graduates of these programs as resource persons and instructors in an attempt to provide appropriate role models for program constituents. A dissemination process providing information related to practices that have been effective in providing psychologically sound and well articulated vocational experiences for culturally diverse handicapped youth should also be provided. Inherent in this process is establishment of validation procedures through demonstration, research, and evaluation.

There is also a need to encourage and provide financial support (federal, local, and private foundations) for institutions that have had a significant track record in developing and implementing educational and vocational programs for bypassed and unserved populations. These institutions (namely, historically Black oriented colleges and selected junior college systems) should be encouraged to conceptualize, develop, and implement vocational efforts for culturally diverse handicapped youth.

Finally, school personnel must broaden their vision and think about the year 2000. Rather than predicting fewer opportunities for employment of handicapped persons, the provision of training opportunities and experiences should enable more and varied employment situations to become realistic options. Discrimination and a lack of attention to the problems of culturally diverse handicapped persons has existed too long. Suggestions and strategies are at hand that will enable more culturally diverse handicapped students to become productive members of society. The knowledge is available. Now the commitment to implementation is needed.

REFERENCES

Adelman, F. W., & Phelps, L. A. Learning to teach handicapped learners. *American Vocational Journal,* 1978, *53*, 27–29.

Halloran, W. D. Handicapped persons: Who are they? *American Vocational Journal,* 1978, *53*, 30–31.

Herbers, J. Changes in society holding Black youth in jobless web. *New York Times,* March 11, 1979, pp. 1:44.

Lee, A. Learning a living across the nation, Volume IV. *Project Baseline.* Flagstaff: Northern Arizona University, October, 1975.

Levitan, S. A., & Taggart, R. *Jobs for the disabled.* Washington DC: George Washington University, Center for Manpower Policy Studies, 1976.

Schwartz, L. An integrated teacher education program for special education—A new approach. *Exceptional Children,* 1967, *33*, 411–416.

Sheppard, G. What research on the mentally retarded has to say. *Journal of Secondary Education,* 1966, *41*, 339–342.

Valverde, L. A. Multicultural education: Social and educational justice. *Educational Leadership,* 1977, *34*, 196–199.

Wells, J. Outside looking in. *Journal of the American Vocational Association,* 1978, *53*, 45–47.

Wright, B. A. *Physical disability—A psychological approach.* New York: Harper & Row, 1960.

Young, H. A., & Young, B. *Retaining Blacks in science: An effective model.* Unpublished paper, University of Louisville, May 1979.

Teacher Education for Culturally Diverse Exceptional Children

by Robert Y. Fuchigami

In 1969 Johnson issued a series of critical comments about the role of special education as a convenient depository by the educational system for nonconforming minority children.

> Special education is part of the arrangement for cooling out students. It has helped to erect a parallel system which permits relief of institutional guilt and humiliation stemming from the failure to achieve competence and effectiveness in the task given to it by society. Special education is helping the regular school maintain its spoiled identity when it creates special programs (whether psychodynamic or behavioral modification) for the "disruptive child" and the "slow learner," many of whom, for some strange reason, happen to be black and poor and live in the inner city. (p. 245)
>
> The message is clear: special education . . . suffers from obsolete, racist conceptions of deviance and unjustifiable ways of cooling children out. . . . However, special education practices do not stand alone. They are joined, in the school context, by a host of additional and related problems, including (a) ability grouping which stops short of special education placement in which minority group students are often placed in the lowest tracks, (b) racist teachers and administrators, or those perceived to be so, (c) proportionately few minority teachers and administrators, (d) a curriculum which fails to give appropriate attention to the history and culture of minority groups, and (e) a curriculum focus upon Anglo middle class values based on the Protestant ethic. (p. 250)

PROGRESS IN MINORITY CONCERNS

In the decade following publication of those comments, special educators have witnessed some significant progress related to minority populations. The passage of Public Law 94-142 was, of course, the most significant event of the decade and most analysts acknowledge that much of the impetus for legislation and its specific requirements were derived from actions and activities of special educators and parents concerned about minority related issues such as inappropriate testing procedures, labeling, disproportionate numbers of culturally diverse children in special classes, inappropriate curricula, and inadequate preparation of teachers and administrators to work with culturally diverse students and parents. An analysis of Public Law 94-142 requirements reveals considerable evidence that minority concerns were carefully considered in developing various provisions of the legislation. Some of the requirements and their implications for culturally diverse groups were described in The Council for Exceptional Children's policy statements on minorities (CEC, 1978):

1. The requirement that tests administered to determine status must be nondiscriminatory effectively limits the power of measurement instruments against minorities in terms of item selection and standardization samples.
2. The provision that no single test may be the basis for placement reduced the likelihood that the typically lowered verbal scores of minority students on IQ measures will determine placement, as has happened too frequently in the past.
3. The requirement that assessment be multidisciplinary and drawn from multiple resources increases the probability that nonverbal strengths of the learner, which are more likely to be demonstrated in the classroom than in the testing situation, will be reported by the teacher and taken into account in planning.
4. The requirement that a parent or surrogate parent participate in planning provides for an advocate for the language needs and cultural values of the minority exceptional learner.
5. The requirement of assignment of the least restrictive alternative should provide assurance against the enforced segregation of minority students in self contained special classrooms, where they have been overrepresented in the past. (p. 60)

In addition to legislative progress that has served as the catalyst for major changes in program operations at the local and state level, special educators have seen significant progress in minority related activites within major professional organizations. For example, The Council for Exceptional Children has established a staff position to focus on minority concerns and issues. CEC also sponsored a national institute and conference on cultural diversity in 1973 and adopted a set of wide ranging policy statements on minorities at the 1978 international convention (CEC, 1978).

Some progress has been made in the area of special education relative to minorities and their concerns. It is hoped that the successful implementation of Public Law 94-142 requirements will bring about some of the needed reforms in educational programing identified by minority personnel. This leaves one major area of concern for minorities: teacher education.

As noted earlier, in 1978 The Council for Exceptional Children adopted a set of policy statements regarding cultural diversity and special education. Among the set of beliefs adopted by the general assembly was one that stated:

> . . . an appropriate public education that meets unique needs of minority children must include careful consideration of cultural and ethnic influences which might affect student performances in areas such as pupil assessment, pupil placement, teaching strategies, curriculum adaptation, and development of instructional materials. (p. 57)

If an appropriate public education for culturally diverse populations is to become a reality, it is critical that persons in positions to deliver that education—teachers and administrators—have the necessary knowledge and skills to teach minority children. There is reason to believe that colleges of education have done less than an adequate job of preparing teachers and administrators for the responsibility. The purpose of this article is to (a) examine some of the issues and concerns in teacher education related to training personnel to work with culturally diverse children, (b) examine several forces influencing change in teacher education programs, and (c) discuss conceptualization issues and several alternative implementation strategies for change.

ISSUES AND CONCERNS IN TEACHER EDUCATION

Minority special educators have identified a wide variety of problems related to the education of culturally diverse children that indirectly indict teacher preparation centers for their inadequacies in preparing teachers and administrators for their respective responsibilities. These problems include (a) a need to change attitudes and expectations, (b) a need to develop some strategies for implementing content, (c) a need to become familiar with existing materials, (d) a need for inservice training of college teaching faculty, and (e) a need for institutional commitment to the idea of including information about minorities in teacher preparation programs.

Changing Teacher Attitudes and Expectations

McLaughlin-Williams (1977) stated the following:

> One reason that nonwhite children are placed in special education in higher percentages than would be expected, compared to their actual numbers in the total population, is inappropriate testing. Another reason is inappropriate teacher expectations. Educators determine

"behavior problems," "disruptive behavior," or "mental retardation" largely on the basis of their own perceptions of acceptable and
unacceptable behavior. Nonwhite pupils are also disadvantaged if
teachers (white or nonwhite) have adopted middle-class values and
norms. Just as beauty exists in the eye of the beholder, so disruptive or
unacceptable behavior, or below-normal achievement, often exists in
the eye of the educator. (p. 111)

Based on such comments, teacher and administrator attitudes and
expectations can be identified as the first issue in teacher education related
to culturally diverse students. In general, it can be stated that negative
attitudes and lowered expectations have led to misreferrals, misdiagnoses,
and misplacements of culturally diverse children into special classes for the
mentally retarded or emotionally disturbed. If attitudes and expectations
are to be altered, colleges of education and district inservice training
programs will need to provide educators with information and skills about
how to teach culturally diverse children and also provide them with opportunities to apply the skills in appropriate field settings.

Developing Strategies to Implement Content

A second issue, which will be discussed later in this article, is a need
for strategies and conceptualizations to implement content related to minorities. Jones and Wilderson (1976) stated the need clearly and concisely:

The present need is to develop conceptualizations which point the
direction for change. This means that we have little need for additional
writings on the inappropriateness of tests for use with minority children; regular teachers do not need to be berated for their lack of
familiarity with important elements of minority cultures and life
styles; school administrators do not need to be told that evaluation
involving minority children will be difficult. Rather, the need is for
conceptualizations, strategies, and techniques which will be useful to
those who assess, teach, and evaluate minority children placed in
mainstream settings. (p. 10)

Familiarizing Teachers with Materials

A third issue is the perceived shortage of teacher training materials
related to culturally diverse children. In a marketing survey conducted in
1978 for The Council for Exceptional Children by Fuchigami, 78% of the
250 colleges and universities that responded reported they did not have
training materials on minority groups. Some schools indicated that their
students could take courses in ethnic studies across campus and thereby be
exposed to information on culturally diverse groups. However, a few
schools candidly admitted that most students did not avail themselves of the
opportunity because course requirements for the teaching credential were

so great they could not add electives to their overcrowded schedules. Contrary to the perceptions of many educators, a search for materials on minorities will reveal a wide variety of information available for teacher trainers developed by Teacher Corps projects, Ethnic Heritage projects, and commercial publishing companies.

Inservice Training for College Faculty

A fourth issue in teacher education is the relative lack of knowledge and expertise about cultural diversity among the faculty in colleges of education. In essence, it is apparent that teacher training faculty members need training themselves about minorities and minority handicapped populations. What is needed are Dean's Grant types of faculty inservice training with a focus on cultural diversity and the minority handicapped population.

Institutional Commitment

A fifth issue is the lack of commitment by colleges of education to provide information about cultural diversity in their teacher preparation programs. Banks (1979) postulated that the primary reason there is so little institutional commitment to providing information about minorities is an ideological one. He believes that American educators are primarily assimilationists who still believe in the melting pot theory of the 1930's. He stated that basic reform cannot take place unless the mainstream assimilationists begin to have personal contact and dialog with pluralistic educators so they can resolve their philosophical disagreements.

FORCES AFFECTING CHANGE IN TEACHER EDUCATION

Dean's Grants

Public Law 94-142 is obviously one of the most significant forces influencing change in teacher education. During the debate on the legislation, both houses of Congress recognized the need for informing special and regular education personnel about the law. In addition, the Bureau of Education for the Handicapped noted the need for educating college faculty members about the law. This need was translated into an action plan for funding known as the Dean's Grant. In a recent document prepared for the American Association of Colleges of Teacher Education (AACTE), Clair, Hagerty, and Merchant (1979) challenged teacher educators to view Public Law 94-142 in a wider context and respond to the opportunity to strengthen the profession as a whole. Basic reform in teacher preparation programs using Public Law 94-142 as a catalyst for change has also been strongly advocated by Meyen (1979), Reynolds (1979), and the National Support System Project based at the University of Minnesota (Grosenick & Reynolds, 1978). During the past 5 years, almost 200 colleges and universities involved in teacher preparation have used Dean's Grants to change prevailing practices toward inclusion of information about exceptional children in their preservice training programs.

Unfortunately, most of the Dean's Grant projects reveal little evidence that information about minority groups is included in projected activities or outcomes. Perhaps teacher educators need to be reminded of the large numbers of culturally diverse children involved. For example, Dunn (1968) stated that in his best judgment:

> . . . about 60 to 80 percent of the pupils taught by special educators are from low status backgrounds including Afro-Americans, American Indians, Mexicans, and Puerto Rican Americans; those from non-standard English speaking, broken, disorganized and inadequate homes, and children from other non middle class environments. (p. 5)

In the absence of more definitive or more recent data, it is estimated that over 30% of the children returning to the regular classroom for the major part of the school day are non White minority handicapped children. Unfortunately, it appears that neither regular nor special educators have received much information about this population in their training programs.

In discussing Dean's Grants, Grosenick and Reynolds (1978) provided a clear reminder of the need to consider the wide ranging aspects of Public Law 94-142 legislation when they stated the following:

> The implementation of such a mandate for change is accompanied, not surprisingly, by an examination of attitudes, skills and competencies, reward systems, and communication among the various groups affected. Such an examination makes it eminently clear that education does not (or should not) operate in a vacuum. In other words, change toward educating handicapped children in the least restrictive environment has social, economic, and political implications in addition to educational ramifications. (p. 7)

The remarks can clearly be interpreted to mean that teacher trainers have a strong responsibility to provide information about culturally diverse groups in their teacher and administrator preparation programs. Given this directive, minority educators and parents will be intensely interested in knowing how responsive and responsible teacher trainers can be.

Teacher Licensing Agencies

A second force affecting teacher education is teacher licensing agencies. In California, the Commission on Teacher Preparation and Licensing requires all teachers and administrators applying for their teaching credential to have a specific set of knowledge and skills related to the education of exceptional children. All higher education teacher preparation centers in California have established either a course or set of courses whereby teachers and administrators are able to meet those requirements. Unfortunately, there is only one requirement in the set that can be interpreted as information related to culturally diverse populations: teachers are required to be able to analyze nondiscriminatory assessment procedures, including a sensitivity to cultural and linguistic factors (Commission on Teacher Preparation and Licensing, 1978).

Teacher Accreditation Groups

A third force affecting teacher education is teacher accreditation groups. The new accreditation standards adopted by the National Council for Accreditation of Teacher Education (NCATE) require all NCATE accredited teacher education programs to include a training component on multicultural education. While the reference to a multicultural education component is included throughout the revised standards document, Section 2,1.1 on multicultural education summarizes the intent:

> Multicultural education is preparation for the social, political, and economic realities that individuals experience in culturally diverse and complex human encounters. These realities have both national and international dimensions. This preparation provides a process by which an individual develops competencies for perceiving, believing, evaluating, and behaving in differential cultural settings. Thus, multicultural education is viewed as an on-going assessment process to help institutions and individuals become more responsible to the human condition, individual cultural integrity, and cultural pluralism in society.
>
> Provision should be made for instruction in multicultural education in teacher education programs. Multicultural education should receive attention in courses, seminars, directed readings, laboratory and clinical experiences, practicum, and other types of field experiences.
>
> Multicultural education could include but not be limited to experiences which: (1) Promote analytical and evaluative abilities to confront issues such as participatory democracy, racism and sexism, and the parity of power; (2) Develop skills for values clarification including the study of manifest and latent transmission of values; (3) Examine the dynamics of diverse cultures and the implications for developing teaching strategies, and (4) Examine linguistic variations and diverse learning styles as a basis for the development of appropriate teaching strategies. Standard: The institution gives evidence of planning for multicultural education in its teacher education curricula including both the general and professional studies components.

The new standards became effective on January 1, 1979. To assist teacher preparation centers, the American Association of Colleges of Teacher Education (AACTE) has been conducting a series of conferences across the nation to help teacher educators learn how to implement the new standards. Unfortunately, AACTE, which is also involved in promoting Dean's Grant projects, has not tried to relate the concern about minorities to their activities in the area of the handicapped.

In addition to trying to meet legislative mandates, state credential licensing requirements, and accreditation standards, teacher educators are expected to attend to professional policy statements adopted by State Boards of Education and professional organizations such as The Council for Exceptional Children. Given the need to respond adequately to all of these forces and others, some teacher trainers are considering the possibilities of a more extended teacher preparation program (Ryan, 1979).

CONCEPTUALIZATION ISSUES AND IMPLEMENTATION STRATEGIES

As mentioned earlier, Jones and Wilderson (1976) identified conceptualizations and strategies relative to the education of culturally diverse handicapped children as among the primary needs of teacher educators at this time. In reviewing the various forces and examining responses of some colleges to them, it appears that teacher trainers are responding to the various mandates and requirements as separate entities requiring separate sets of modules or courses.

Interrelating Minority Concerns with Other Groups

Perhaps it is time to consider the possibility of combining the requirements or at least recognizing that there is considerable overlap in concerns and issues relative to conditions of exceptionality and ethnicity. Some comments from Teacher Corps training materials (Gold, Grant, & Rivlin, 1977) help illustrate the similarities in issues and concern.

1. Respect for diversity is fundamental, for without it all those who are different are excluded from full participation in our society.
2. A pluralistic society is totally compatible with America's highest ideals. To the extent that pluralism is realized, all people may retain a healthy ethnic pride, an abiding sense of their own culture, and a respect for and appreciation of the people and individuals from ethnically and culturally different heritages.
3. Our goal must be to develop commitment to the principle that to be different is not to be inferior, that one may be different and equal at the same time.

4. A child's coming from a cultural background different from that of the teacher, or from that of most of the other children in the class, is not automatically a handicap.

5. A first step is to become aware of labels that hide as much or more than they reveal.

6. . . . all children want to know that they are accepted as people and are not ridiculed either publicly or privately. They all want to feel the thrill of success, even though they may vary in the degree to which they want this success to be acknowledged publicly.

7. The approach to another culture is either a positive one of willingness to accept what is different or a negative one of conscious or unconscious fear and rejection.

8. . . . teachers should not forget that they teach individuals and not ethnic groups. Nor can teachers afford to ignore Kant's dictum, "so live as to treat every individual as an end in himself, not as a means to an end."(p. 17)

The relationship of issues and concerns relative to minorities and the handicapped was clearly recognized by Carl Grant (1977) who discussed those mutual interests in terms of multicultural education in the following way:

> In order to truly recognize, accept, and affirm cultural diversity and individual differences, it is essential that we adopt an overriding educational philosophy that respects the cultural and individual differences of all people, regardless of their racial, ethnic, cultural or religious backgrounds, or physical differences. The belief that all people must be accorded respect is undergirded by a fundamental acceptance of the premise that all people have intrinsic worth. It should thus be the goal of society's socializing institution—especially our schools—to recognize the worth of all people and to instill and maintain the importance of equal respect for all. Educational policies and practices which respect and affirm cultural diversity and individual differences are needed for achieving this goal. In theory and practice, we must have Education that is Multi-Cultural. (p. 65)

It would appear at this time that Teacher Corps trainers may have a better grasp of the interrelationship of various minority groups in our society than do special educators. As conceptualizations and strategies are considered, their materials and inherent experiences should be reviewed.

Alternatives for Imparting Information about Cultural Diversity

Alternative approaches that a college might consider for preparing prospective teachers to teach culturally diverse handicapped pupils include: (a) a separate module or course, (b) a series of courses, (c) general diffusion of information throughout the training program, or (d) experimental courses.

A separate module or course. The idea of a separate module or course is appealing but Fuchigami (1979) noted the limitations of this approach.

> Equitability in coverage basically refers to equal coverage for groups studied in the course. Most of you are familiar with the lack of equal coverage in your education relative to western civilizations versus eastern civilizations or the attention given Europe versus the attention given Asia in your history and philosophy course. The same imbalance tends to occur whenever a course is established on multicultural education. The emphasis is on Blacks—especially if a Black is teaching, or the emphasis is on Chicanos if a Mexican American is in charge. Since Asian Americans are rarely involved in the teaching of such courses, the Asian American issues and concerns are usually minimized or not presented. Fortunately, the American Indian is included even though their numbers are comparable to the Asian American population in this nation. In essence, Asian American concerns and issues are frequently minimized or overlooked in multicultural courses and this is particularly evident when colleges and universities offer a single course related to multicultural education.

The problems would be compounded if issues and concerns related to exceptional children were added to the course. It is evident that offering a single course on human and cultural diversity is a less than adequate response for colleges to consider in preparing teachers and administrators to work with minority and culturally diverse handicapped children.

A series of courses. A set of courses on minorities and culturally diverse handicapped children is somewhat more appealing. For example, the Office of Intergroup Relations of the California State Department of Education recently identified six areas of content to be included in a sound multicultural education training program for teachers and administrators. The six areas, each of which could be the basis for a separate course, are as follows:

1. Root cultures from which American ethnic groups have developed.
2. United States experience of various ethnic groups.
3. Changing cultures of ethnic groups.
4. Relations with the rest of society.
5. Current situation of ethnic groups.
6. Future of ethnic groups.

Fuchigami (1979) indicated how each of the areas could be the basis for a separate course:

> For example, a course on cultural heritage and cultural awareness involving cross cultural concepts could be developed to examine the root cultures of various American ethnic groups. Another course would have a historical focus to examine the varied United States experience of ethnic groups. A third course would focus on concepts

such as assimilation and the melting pot versus amalgamation and the salad bowl with an examination of how different ethnic groups were either assimilated or excluded based on color, race, or religion. A fourth course could be developed with an emphasis on human and intergroup relations including relations within groups and between groups. A fifth course could focus on the current situation of various ethnic groups. In this course individual ethnic members would attempt to assess the degree to which they have retained, assimilated, amalgamated, and/or rejected values, customs, and mores of previous generations of their groups. A sixth course would focus on the future of ethnic groups in America. In this course each group of ethnic individuals would be asked to decide what elements, values, artifacts, customs, and mores of previous generations it would like to see retained, assimilated, amalgamated, and/or rejected. Following this type of exercise, the outcomes of the decision making process could be further examined in terms of whether they are in conflict with other ethnic and racial groups. Finally such a course could examine areas of conflict and discuss conflict resolving alternatives.

Appraising the probability of getting approval and commitment by teacher preparation centers for such a set of courses, Fuchigami (1979) concluded:

> In reality, however, it is my opinion that none of California's colleges and universities involved in training of teachers and administrators will establish separate courses as ideally presented. In fact, most will try to do everything in a single course and cover all of the visible minority groups such as the Blacks, Chicanos, Asian Americans, Native American Indians, and probably add women and the handicapped.

General diffusion of information. The third alternative is to take the information about minorities and culturally diverse handicapped populations and integrate it throughout the training program wherever it might be appropriate. This would be an ideal but complex approach and it would be difficult to implement without all faculty being knowledgeable about different groups of students. It is, however, the approach that is most desirable in terms of getting the entire faculty involved in issues and concerns related to minorities and culturally diverse handicapped children. For example, in a Dean's Grant report, McLaughlin-Williams (1977) commented:

> Children in special education vary physically, psychologically, and/or academically from society's "norm." In addition to these differences, exceptional nonwhite children vary socially and culturally from white children, handicapped or normal. If, as Birch (1974) stated, "mainstreaming is providing high-quality special education to exceptional children while they remain in regular classes for as much of the day as possible," then one must consider ethnic and cultural aspects when mainstreaming a nonwhite child. (p. 107)

Some critical factors that must be examined for their implications for culturally diverse exceptional children are: (a) staff attitudes, (b) placement procedures, (c) curriculum, (d) preparation of parents, (e) preparation of peers, (f) preparation of the culturally diverse special child, and (g) implementation procedure.

McLaughlin-Williams proceeded to discuss each of the factors in detail.

The integration of the type of information developed by minority educators such as McLaughlin-Williams (1976); Banks (1975); Noar (1974); Jones (1976); and Bransford, Baca, and Lane (1974) will help both the college of education faculty and their students ultimately improve the education of minority and culturally diverse exceptional children in regular and special education. The information could be integrated into a wide variety of courses such as educational psychology, history and philosophy of education, tests and measurements, educational foundations, curriculum courses, and counseling courses. Unfortunately, the probability of getting all faculty involved in this type of alternative is very low regardless of its desirability.

Experimental courses. A fourth alternative is to develop some experimental courses in human and cultural diversity incorporating some of the concepts and materials developed by the Teacher Corps, Ethnic Heritage Projects, and the American Association of Colleges of Teacher Education (AACTE). The previously mentioned conceptualization of a multicultural education developed by Carl Grant (1977) is particularly important and should be pursued. When his concepts are incorporated into a set of classroom activities as they were by Gloria Grant and her associates in the Teacher Corps publication, *In Praise of Diversity* (Grant, 1977), one can easily see the mutual interests and concerns shared by such groups as the elderly, women, racial groups, and handicapped people. Special educators who begin to explore the possibilities of joint ventures with other groups who have also had to deal with problems such as labeling, stereotyping, and discrimination will find themselves making some significant and exciting breakthroughs in traditional ways of thinking. As rapidly as possible, the experimental courses combining human and cultural diversity should become required courses in teacher and administrator training programs. Such courses would also be valuable for students majoring in psychology or educational psychology.

CONCLUSION

Public Law 94-142 is having a remarkable and significant impact on educational practices programs including teacher preparation programs. In this article, it was pointed out that because so many of the children being mainstreamed into regular classrooms are culturally diverse children, it is imperative that colleges and local school districts providing preservice and inservice training move rapidly toward inclusion of information about minorities and culturally diverse handicapped students in their personnel training activities. Perspectives on the issue and some alternatives for implementation were presented.

McLaughlin-Williams (1977) stated the dream of minority educators when she said:

> Mainstreaming can become a force for the valuing of individual differences, a process to foster acceptance of varying physical, psychological, educational, and racial characteristics, and a futuristic model to celebrate variance as a desirable state. Mainstreaming can be likened to a tributary flowing into a river: Some portions are smooth and placid; others are swift and contain rapids, protuberances, and obstacles; and still others are so difficult passage is tenuous and uncertain, perhaps impossible. If the special education tributary is eventually to flow into the educational mainstream, all barriers must be removed. (p. 107)

A major barrier is a teacher education program that fails to provide information and skills about how to work with minority students and their parents. In essence, minority children must not be expected to carry the burden of teacher and administrator ignorance about minorities into the 1980's. Teacher trainers have an opportunity and a directive to make the necessary changes. The question remains: How will they respond?

REFERENCES

Banks, J. A. *Teaching strategies for ethnic studies*. Boston: Allyn & Bacon, 1975.

Banks, J. A. *Multiethnic/multicultural teacher education: Conceptual, historical, and ideological issues*. Paper presented at the Institutes on Multiethnic Studies for Teacher Education sponsored by the American Association of Colleges of Teacher Education, San Francisco, April 1979.

Bransford, L., Baca, L., & Lane, K. *Cultural diversity and the exceptional child*. Reston VA: The Council for Exceptional Children, 1974.

Clair, J., Hagerty, G., & Merchant, D. *Redesign for teacher education: Assistance for the planning of Dean's Grant projects*. Washington DC: American Association of Colleges of Teacher Education, 1979.

Commission on Teacher Preparation and Licensing. *Guidelines for developing special education training for teachers and administrators*. Sacramento CA: Author, 1978.

The Council for Exceptional Children. Minorities position policy statements. *Exceptional Children,* 1978, *45*, 57–64.

Dunn, L. M. Special education for the mildly retarded—Is much of it justifiable? *Exceptional Children,* 1968, *35*, 5–22.

Fuchigami, R. Y. *Perspectives on teacher training for desegregation and cultural diversity:* Some issues and concerns. Paper presented at the National Association of Asian American and Pacific Education Conference, April, 1979.

Gold, M. J., Grant, C. A., & Rivlin, H. N. *In praise of cultural diversity.* Washington DC: Teacher Corps and Association of Teacher Educators, 1977.

Grant, C. A. Education that is multicultural and P/C BTE: Discussion and recommendations for teacher education. *Pluralism and the American teacher.* Washington DC: Ethnic Heritage Center for Teacher Education, American Association of Colleges of Teacher Education, 1977.

Grant, G. *In praise of diversity: Multicultural applications.* Omaha: Teacher Corps, Center for Urban Education, University of Nebraska at Omaha, 1977.

Grosenick, J., & Reynolds, M. *Teacher education: Renegotiating roles for mainstreaming.* Reston VA: The Council for Exceptional Children, 1978.

Johnson, J. L. Special education in the inner city: A change for the future or another means for cooling the mark off? *Journal of Special Education,* 1969, *3*, 241–251.

Jones, R. L., & Wilderson, F. B. *Mainstreaming and the minority child.* Reston VA: The Council for Exceptional Children, 1976.

McLaughlin-Williams J. The implications of mainstreaming for nonwhite children. In Bates, P., West, T.L., & Schmerl, R.B. (Eds.). *Mainstreaming: Problems, potentials, and perspectives.* Minneapolis MN: National Support Systems Project, 1977.

Meyen, E. L. Mainstreaming colleges of education. *Teacher Education and Special Education,* 1979, *2*, 5–8.

National Council for Accreditation of Teacher Education. *Standards for accreditation of teacher education.* Washington DC: Author, 1979.

Noar, G. *The teacher and integration.* Washington DC: National Education Association, 1974.

Reynolds, M. A look to the future in teacher education. *Teacher Education and Special Education,* 1979, *2*, 9–11.

Ryan, K. *Mainstreaming: The last straw.* Paper presented at the Conference on Dean's Grants, University of Minnesota, Minneapolis, May 1979.

Part II
Sources
of Information

- Agencies and Centers
- Desegregation Assistance Centers and Training Institutes
- Teacher-Training Programs
- Bilingual/Bicultural Special Education Training Projects
- Directory of Persons
- Networks
- Indexes, Databases, Journals, and Newsletters

Funding Agencies to Contact for Bilingual Special Education Grants

Bureau of Occupational and Adult Education
Division of Research & Development
400 Maryland Ave, SW
Washington, DC 20202

Bilingual Vocational Instructor Training Program

Office of Bilingual Education and Minority Languages Affairs
400 Maryland Ave, SW
Washington, DC 20202

Bilingual Education Training Grants; Bilingual Education Fellowships (Doctoral); Bilingual Education Dean's Grant (College of Education)

Office of Indian Education
FOB 6, 400 Maryland Ave, SW
Washington, DC 20202

Indian Education Training (Special Projects); Indian Education Fellowships

Office of Special Education
US Department of Education
Regional Office Bldg, 7th & D Sts, SW
Washington, DC 20202

Personnel Training for the Education of the Handicapped: Higher Education and Public School Program Grants

Teacher Centers—Director
400 Maryland Ave, SW, Rm 2130
Washington, DC 20202

Development of programs in mainstreaming, inservice education, etc.

Editors' Note: Individual states have Federal Formula Grants with certain percentages used for teacher training. Inquire at your State Department of Education for further information.

Special Education/ Handicapped Agencies*

Association for Children with Learning Disabilities (ACLD)
5225 Grace St
Pittsburgh, PA 15236

Provides information to increase public understanding of the needs of children with learning disabilities, including facts on federal legislation for special education for children with learning disabilities. National organization sponsors programs and an annual conference. Local chapters work to promote programs in schools to meet the needs of learning-disabled children. Individuals may join. Monthly newsletter, directory of organizations and schools, and a list of publications are available.

Association for Children with Retarded Mental Development, Inc
902 Broadway
New York, NY 10010

Promotes development of all levels of services for mentally retarded persons. Provides educational, rehabilitative, recreational, and residential services. Concerned with educational issues of centralization, mainstreaming, and regional program implementation. Current programs include activities for daily living, work study programs, and sheltered workshops. Maintains speakers' bureaus, organizes activities for local groups, and represents lay groups before government groups. Publications are available.

AVKO Educational and Research Foundation, Inc
3084 Willard Rd
Birch Run, MI 48415

Conducts research in reading and spelling with emphasis on developing practical materials and techniques. Suggests that children with learning disabilities or dyslexia can be taught to read and that parents play a vital role in a child's education. Advocates that school systems provide training for parents to help children with learning problems and typewriting programs for those with learning problems. Free catalogs.

---

*Reprinted from Bilingual Special Education Packet. Rosslyn, VA: National Clearinghouse for Bilingual Education, 1981.

Center on Human Policy
216 Ostrom Ave
Syracuse, NY 13210

Promotes integration of disabled into society and monitors quality of human services. Provides special education information, advocacy consultation and resources, legal rights information, and community education strategies. Serves parents' groups and national organizations. School workshops, books, slide shows, posters, and children's stories are available.

Center for Law and Education, Inc
Gutman Library—6 Appian Way
Cambridge, MA 02138

Gives advice and referrals to local legal service agencies regarding education programs such as race and sex discrimination, special education, bilingual-bicultural education, discipline and student rights, and competency testing. Works primarily with individuals and groups already being served by a local legal service program. Serves education advocacy organizations and parents' groups around the country. Publications and information are available free to low-income individuals and groups.

Children's Defense Fund
1520 New Hampshire Ave
Washington, DC 20036

Provides long-range and systematic advocacy of institutional reforms and changes in policy affecting children. Current issues include education-excluded or misclassified children and comprehensive child development services. Action includes litigation, research, federal policy monitoring, negotiation, and public information. Maintains Children's Public Policy Network (call toll free: 800-424-9602). Gives information and technical assistance to community groups and assistance with PL 94-142 and Section 504. Advocacy handbook and publications are available on children's health, civil rights, child care, and special education.

Clearinghouse on the Handicapped
Office of Special Education and Rehabilitative Services
Rm 3106, Switzer Bldg
Washington, DC 20202

Coordinates efforts of federal agencies on behalf of handicapped individuals. Provides information to the public on services and programs. Identifies gaps in services and encourages development of new services. Free 400-page directory of concerned national organizations.

Closer Look
1201 16th St, NW, Suite 606E
Washington, DC 20036

National information center for parents of children with handicaps. Helps prospective special education teachers and professionals. Provides information on parent organizing, testing, and evaluation. Publications and journals are available.

Committee on Diagnostic Reading Tests, Inc
Mountain Home, NC 28758

Seeks to improve teaching of reading skills by providing refresher courses and work conferences to individuals. Serves schools, colleges, organizations, and persons concerned with teaching reading and language skills. Test materials and other publications are available.

Conference of Executives of American Schools for the Deaf
5043 Wisconsin Ave, NW
Washington, DC 20016

Responds to inquiries about deafness with organizational programs, teachers, administrators, activities, and captioned films. A journal and other publications are available.

Coordinating Council for Handicapped Children
(Parent Information Center)
407 S Dearborn St, Rm 680
Chicago, IL 60605

Provides information on the legal rights of handicapped children to parents and professionals, parent training workshops, advocacy, and referral services. Operates Parent Information Center, which is affiliated with Closer Look. Publications and fact sheets on laws and tax deductions are available.

The Council for Exceptional Children Information Center
1920 Association Dr
Reston, VA 22091

Provides technical assistance and training for those involved with exceptional children. Conducts short- and long-term consultation and studies. Programs include speakers, conferences, workshops, customized searches and products, and self-instructional packages. Journals and books are available.

Education Development Center
55 Chapel St
Newton, MA 02160

Seeks to further educational and social development through curriculum reform and institutional development. Programs address desegregation, the handicapped, quantitative skills, continuing education, sexism, and bilingual education. A guide to programs is available.

Educational Due Process Services
Box 57387
Washington, DC 20037

Provides consultation and technical assistance in response to Part I of PL 94-142, the Education for All Handicapped Children Act. Information clearinghouse, training materials, and the Special Education Due Process Hearing Stimulation package have been used by educational agencies and university classes.

Educational Facilities Laboratories
850 Third Ave
New York, NY 10022

Acts as liaison between community planners and facilities managers to help educational facilities meet community needs. Researches and disseminates information on public service institutions for education, recreation, health care, and the arts. Currently working on enrollment decline and surplus space, energy conservation, and accessibility for the handicapped. Reports and films are available.

Home and School Institute, Inc
c/o Trinity College
Washington, DC 20017

Develops working partnerships between families and community support systems. With human service agencies and schools, designs staff training and special family curricula, such as Project Help (a home-based learning program), services to children with handicaps, and Title I training. With families, works to strengthen parenting and improve family health and well-being. Publications on home learning techniques are available. (Send stamped, self-addressed envelope with requests for information.)

Humanics
881 Peachtree St, NE
Atlanta, GA 30309

Provides training and information services to individuals and to educational and community agencies. Interested in strengthening parent involvement and in improving services. Offers workshops on delivering social services, implementing policies, and building parent involvement. Tuition is charged for workshops. Publications include books on parent involvement, social services, education, and special education geared to parents and teachers.

International Association of Parents of the Deaf
814 Thayer Ave
Silver Spring, MD 20910

Information and referral service for parents and the general public. Compiles position papers, lists of speakers, and reading materials. Publishes a newsletter.

†Latino Institute, Research Division
Project REACHH
1760 Reston Ave, Suite 101
Reston, VA 22090

Project REACHH is a recently funded project established by the Office of Special Education in the US Department of Education to the Latino Institute Research Division to produce a state-of-the-art monograph on the education of Hispanic

---

†Added by the editors.

handicapped children. Input—special reports, research papers, recent publications, or any other documentation that might be included in bibliographic entries and review of the literature—is being sought from researchers, practitioners, and local service agencies.

†Multicultural Special Education Network (MUSEP)
Contact Person: Dr. Leonard Baca
School of Education, Campus Box 249
University of Colorado
Boulder, CO 80309

Designed to create a cooperative training and technical assistance network in the Western region for bilingual special education project personnel. Staff personnel are involved with Hispanic, American Indian, and Asian populations. Conducts needs assessment surveys, literature reviews, and evaluation activities. Quarterly newsletter reports the activities of the project.

National Association for the Deaf-Blind
2703 Forest Oak Circle
Norman, OK 73071

Promotes the health, education, and welfare of deaf-blind children, youth, and adults. Advocates new ideas and techniques in dealing with the deaf-blind. Disseminates information through conferences and publications.

National Association for Retarded Citizens
2709 Ave E East
Arlington, TX 76011

Evaluates and monitors services for retarded citizens. Serves state and local associations. Seeks prevention of mental retardation through known methods, trains citizen advocates, and obtains free public educational opportunities for the retarded. On-the-job training programs, financial assistance to students of mental retardation, and legal assistance are available. Disseminates newsletter to prospective employers encouraging the hiring of clients.

National Center for Law and the Deaf
7th St & Florida Ave, NE
Washington, DC 20002

Represents the hearing-impaired in lawsuits concerning employment, education, receipt of government or social service, and insurance discrimination. Assists legislative writing, offers educational workshops on legislation and regulations, advocates television captioning, monitors hearing-aid sales practices, offers course on law and the deaf, and helps deaf students attend law school. Documents and a newsletter are available.

---

†Added by the editors.

National Easter Seal Society for Crippled Children and Adults, Inc
2023 W Ogden Ave
Chicago, IL 60612

Provides a wide variety of services to physically handicapped: rehabilitation, advocacy, research, education, organization, and funding. Serves the physically handicapped and their families, rehabilitation workers, teachers, students, volunteers—all those who seek practical or technical information concerning physical handicaps and adaptation to them. Maintains reference service and publishes resource packets and bibliographies.

National School Volunteer Program
300 N Washington St
Alexandria, VA 22314

Promotes the creative involvement of school volunteers and seeks to create a partnership between educators and citizens through organized school volunteer service programs. Also concerned with broadening community support for education, desegregation, business/education cooperation, expanding opportunities for older Americans, and handicapped education. Provides national and regional conferences and publishes various materials, including annotated bibliographies of school volunteer materials and a monthly newsletter.

National Society for Autistic Children
1234 Massachusetts Ave, NW, Suite 1017
Washington, DC 20005

Provides information and referral service and local chapter structure. Serves parents, professionals, students, libraries, schools and universities, and governments.

Native American Rights Fund
506 Broadway
Boulder, CO 80302

Promotes tribal life and resources, human rights, accountability of policymakers, and the effective and orderly development of Indian law. The Indian Education Legal Support project deals with desegregation, bilingualism, and special education. Serves tribal groups and national Indian organizations.

†Parent Advocacy Coalition for Educational Rights
PACER Center, Inc
4701 Chicago Ave S
Minneapolis, MN 55407

Operates a bilingual parent training program begun in St. Paul. Services are available for parents of Hispanic handicapped children. Assistance is also available for organizations in other states that wish to form coalitions for parent training. Publishes the newsletter *Pacesetter*.

---

†Added by the editors.

President's Committee on Employment of the Handicapped
1111 20th St, NW
Washington, DC 20210

Works to create a climate of acceptance of the handicapped in the work force. Major concern is lack of educational, vocational, and industrial arts training for handicapped citizens. Provides information, materials, and guidance to individuals and groups. Other issues of concern include employment assistance, job placement, training programs, and accessibility of buildings to handicapped people. Many brochures, handbooks, and publications are available.

National and Regional Centers

NATIONAL EVALUATION, DISSEMINATION, AND ASSESSMENT CENTERS

Evaluation, Dissemination, and Assesssment Center
Lesley College
49 Washington Ave
Cambridge, MA 02140
(617) 492-0505

Languages: Greek, Italian, Chinese, Korean, Japanese, Spanish, French, Portuguese, Indochinese Languages
Service Area 1: Education Regions I, II, III and IV (Connecticut, Maine, Massachusetts, New Hampshire, Rhode Island, Vermont, New York, New Jersey, Puerto Rico, Virgin Islands, Delaware, District of Columbia, Maryland, Pennsylvania, Virginia, West Virginia, Alabama, Florida, Georgia, Kentucky, Mississippi, North Carolina and Tennessee)

National Center for the Development of Bilingual Education
Dallas Independent School District
3700 Ross Ave, Box 103
Dallas, TX 75204
(214) 742-5991

Languages: Spanish, Native American Languages
Service Area 2: Education Regions V, VI, VII, and VIII (Illinois, Indiana, Minnesota, Michigan, Ohio, Wisconsin, Iowa, Kansas, Missouri, Nebraska, Arkansas, Louisiana, New Mexico, Oklahoma, Texas, Colorado, Montana, North Dakota, South Dakota, Utah, and Wyoming)

Evaluation, Dissemination, and Assessment Center
California State University at Los Angeles
5151 State University Dr
Los Angeles, CA 90032
(213) 224-3676

Languages: Spanish, Chinese, Pacific Asian Languages
Service Area 3: Education Regions IX and X (Arizona, California, Hawaii,

Nevada, American Samoa, Guam, Trust Territory of the Pacific Islands, Commonwealth of the Northern Mariana Islands, Alaska, Idaho, Oregon, and Washington)

REGIONAL BILINGUAL EDUCATION SERVICE CENTERS

New England Bilingual Education Consortium
345 Blackstone Blvd, Potter Bldg
Providence, RI 02906
(401) 274-9548

Languages: Portuguese, Spanish, Italian, French, Haitian Creole, Cape Verdean, Japanese, Hmong, Vietnamese, Lao, Cambodian, Armenian, Passamaquoddy, Hebrew, Korean, Cantonese, Polish, and Greek
Service Area 1: Rhode Island, Connecticut, Massachusetts, New Hampshire, Vermont, and Maine

Georgetown University Bilingual Education Service Center
DC Transit Bldg, Suite 376
3520 Prospect St, NW
Washington, DC 20007
(202) 625-3540

Languages: Spanish, Vietnamese, Chinese, Greek, Italian, Japanese, Mohawk, Seneca, Haitian Creole
Service Area 2: New York (excluding New York City, and Suffolk and Nassau Counties in New York State), New Jersey, Pennsylvania, Delaware, District of Columbia, Maryland, Virginia, and West Virginia

C. W. Post Bilingual Education Service Center
Hunter College
440 E 26th St, 8th Fl
New York, NY 10010
(212) 481-5070

Languages: Spanish, Italian, French, Russian
Service Area 3: New York City and Suffolk and Nassau Counties in New York State

South Atlantic Bilingual Education Service (SABES) Center
Florida International University
Bay Vista Campus
North Miami, FL 33181
(305) 940-5640

Languages: Spanish, Vietnamese, Portuguese, Russian, Miccosukee, Seminole, Haitian Creole, Arabic, German, Cambodian, Thai, Korean
Service Area 4: Florida, Georgia, South Carolina, and North Carolina

National Bilingual Education Service Center
University of Southwestern Louisiana
PO Box 43410, Allen Hall
Lafayette, LA 70504
(318) 231-6991

Languages: French, Italian, Spanish, Hungarian, Vietnamese, Greek, Haitian Creole
Service Area 5: Louisiana, Mississippi, Alabama, Arkansas, and Tennessee

Bilingual Education Service Center
500 Dwyer Ave
Arlington Heights, IL 60005
(321) 870-4100

Languages: Spanish, Arabic, Oneida, Vietnamese, Objiwa, Lao, Native American Languages
Service Area 6: Michigan, Wisconsin, Minnesota, Indiana, Ohio, Kentucky, Illinois, Iowa, and Missouri

Bilinguals Unified for Educational Opportunities (BUENO)
Education Bldg, Campus Box 249
University of Colorado
Boulder, CO 80309
(303) 492-5416

Languages: Spanish, Vietnamese, Lao
Service Area 7: Colorado, Wyoming, Utah, Kansas, Nebraska, South Dakota, North Dakota, Montana (excluding the Navajo language groups in Colorado and all Native American language groups in Utah)

Bilingual Resource Center
Education Service Center, Region XIII
7703 Lamar Blvd
Austin, TX 78752
(512) 458-9131

Languages: Spanish, Indochinese Languages
Service Area 8: Oklahoma (excluding Native American language groups) and Education Service Center Regions V-XIV, XVI, and XVII in Texas

Bilingual Education Service Center
Intercultural Development Research Associates
5835 Callaghan Rd, Suite 350
San Antonio, TX 78228
(512) 684-8180

Languages: Spanish, Vietnamese, Lao, Cambodian, French

Service Area 9: Education Service Center Regions III, IV, XV, XVIII, and XX in Texas

Rio Grande Border Bilingual Education Service Center
1900 W Schunior
Edinburg, TX 78539
(512) 383-5611

Language: Spanish
Service Area 10: Education Service Center Regions I and II in Texas

Bilingual Education Service Center
National Institute for Multicultural Education
3010 Monte Vista, NE, Suite 203
Albuquerque, NM 87106
(505) 262-1721

Language: Spanish
Service Area 11: New Mexico (excluding Native American language groups) and Education Service Center Region XIX in Texas

Bilingual Education Service Center
San Diego State University
6363 Alvarado Ct, Suite 200
San Diego, CA 92120
(714) 265-5193

Languages: Spanish, Pilipino, Vietnamese, Portuguese
Service Area 12: Arizona, San Diego, Imperial, Riverside, San Bernardino, Kern, San Luis Obispo, and Santa Barbara Counties in California; Clark County in Nevada (excluding Native American language groups in these states)

Bilingual Education Service Center
California State University at Fullerton
800 N State College Blvd
Library, Rm 230
Fullerton, CA 92634
(714) 773-3994

Languages: Spanish, Portuguese, Hmong, Korean, Samoan, Japanese, Pilipino, Vietnamese, Armenian, Cambodian, Thai, Iloco, Cantonese, Mandarin, Tagalog
Service Area 13: Los Angeles, Ventura, and Orange Counties in California (excluding Native American language groups in these counties)

Cross Cultural Resource Center
California State University
Department of Anthropology TKK

6000 J St
Sacramento, CA 95819
(916) 454-6236

Languages; Cantonese, Japanese, Korean, Native American Languages, Punjabi
Service Area 14: Del Norte, Siskiyou, Modoc, Lassen, Shasta, Trinity, Humboldt, Mendocino, Tehama, Plumas, Butte, Glenn, Lake, Colusa, Yolo, Sutter, Yuba, Placer, Nevada, Sierra, El Dorado, Amador, Sacramento, Marin, Sonoma, Napa, and Solano Counties in California; all counties in Nevada (except Clark County and excluding Native American language groups); Douglas, Coos, Curry, Josephine, Jackson, Klamath, Leak, Harne, and Malheur Counties in Oregon; Commonwealth of Northern Mariana Islands; Trust Territories of the Pacific; Guam; American Samoa; and Hawaii

Bilingual Education Service Center
Babel, Inc
255 East 14th St
Oakland, CA 94606
(415) 451-0511

Languages: Spanish, Chinese, Punjabi, Tagalog, Vietnamese
Service Area 15: Contra Costa, San Joaquin, Calaveras, Alphine, Tuolumne, Mono, San Mateo, Alameda, Santa Cruz, Santa Clara, Stanislaus, Mariposa, Monterey, San Benito, Merced, Fresno, Madera, Inyo, Kings, San Francisco, and Tulare Counties in California (excluding Native American language groups in these counties)

Bilingual Education Service Center for Alaska and the Northwest
(BESCAN)
University District Bldg
1107 NE 45th St, Suite 515
Seattle, WA 98105
(206) 543-9424

Languages: Spanish, Russian, Native Alaskan Languages, Chinese, Japanese, Korean, Pilipino, Vietnamese, Pacific Island Languages, Thai
Service Area 16: Washington; Idaho; Alaska; and Clatsop, Columbia, Tillamook, Multnomah, Hood River, Wasco, Sherman, Gilliam, Morrow, Umatilla, Union, Wallowa, Baker, Grant, Wheeler, Crook, Jefferson, Marion, Pok, Lincoln, Benton, Deschutes, Yamhill, Clackamas, Linn, Lane, and Washington Counties in Oregon

Caribbean Bilingual Education Service Center
Avenida Barbosa 609
Esquina Mayaguez
Edificio Sunny Isles, 1st Fl
Hato Rey, PR 00917
(809) 763-3180

Languages: English, Spanish
Service Area 17: Puerto Rico and the Virgin Islands

American Indian Bilingual Education Center
University of New Mexico
College of Education
Albuquerque, NM 87131
(505) 277-3551

Languages: Native American Languages
Service Area 18: Navajo group in Arizona, Colorado, Utah, and all Native American language groups in New Mexico and Oklahoma

Bilingual Education Service Center
Arizona State University
Dixie Gammage Bldg, Rm 258
Tempe, AZ 85281
(602) 965-5688

Languages: Papago, Pima, Hualapai, Supai, Hopi, Ute
Service Area 19: Native American language groups in Arizona, Utah, Nevada, and the counties in California in service areas 12, 13, and 15 above (excluding the Navajo language groups in Arizona and Utah)

Desegregation Assistance Centers and Training Institutes

Funded by Title IV to ensure the civil rights of students, these centers and institutes provide curriculum materials and training for elementary and secondary personnel in an attempt to promote cultural awareness and to supply information about nondiscrimination in the classroom. In addition to these functions, the centers act as referral and/or counseling agencies for school systems needing special materials or services not readily available in specific locales.

Arizona

University of Arizona
Tucson, AZ 85721

William W. Beck
College of Education
Education Bldg
(602) 626-1461

Myra Dinnerstein
Women's Studies
Modern Language 269
(602) 626-4477

California

Bay Area Bilingual Education
League
255 E 14th St
Oakland, CA 94606

Maria Elena Riddle
(415) 451-0511

Far West Laboratory for Educational Resources and Development
1855 Folsom St
San Francisco, CA 94103

Leonard C. Beckum
(415) 565-3079

Lisa Hunter
(415) 565-3110

Los Angeles Foundation
California State University
5151 State University Dr
Los Angeles, CA 90032

Raymond Terrell
(213) 224-3784

Project EQUITY
California State University—
Fullerton
800 N State College Blvd
Fullerton, CA 92634

Dr. Barbara Peterson
(714) 773-3329

San Diego State University
    Foundation
5300 Campanile
San Diego, CA 92182

Alberto M. Ochoa
(714) 265-6656

Social/Philosophical Foundations
California State University—
    Northridge
18111 Nordhoff St
Northridge, CA 91330

Dudley A. Blake
(213) 885-3652

University of California—
    Berkeley
Sponsored Projects/Board of
    Regents
M-11 Wheeler Hall
Berkeley, CA 94720

Lawrence Lowery
(415) 642-8420

University of Santa Clara
Santa Clara, CA 95053

JoAnn Vasquez
The Alameda
(408) 984-4693

or

Division of Continuing
    Education
Bannan Hall 261
(408) 984-4518

Colorado

University of Colorado
Denver, CO 80202
School of Education
1100 14th St

Gretchen Groth
(303) 629-2663

Connecticut

Equity House Incorporated
New England Equal Education
    Center
PO Box 558
South Windsor, CT 06074

John Giordano
(203) 522-7166

District of Columbia

American University
School of Education
Washington, DC 20016

Dr. Sherly Denbo
Dr. David Sadker
3301 New Mexico Ave, NW
(202) 686-3511

Myra Sadker
Massachusetts & Nebraska
    Aves, NW
(202) 686-2186

Florida

University of Miami
School of Education & Allied
    Professions
PO Box 248065
Coral Gables, FL 33124

Dr. Rita Bornstein
(305) 284-3213

Rosa Castro Feinberg
Gordon Foster
(305) 284-3213

Illinois

Northeastern Illinois University
College of Education
5500 N St Louis Ave
Chicago, IL 60625

Dr. George Grimes
(312) 583-4050

Indiana

Indiana University Foundation
School of Education
3951 N Meridian
Indianapolis, IN 46208

Dr. Herman Norman
(317) 264-2921

Kansas

Kansas State University
College of Education
Department of Administration
    Foundation
Holton Hall
Manhattan, KS 66506

Charles I. Rankin
(913) 532-6408

Louisiana

Grambling State University
College of Education

PO Box 46
Grambling, LA 71245

Dr. Burnett Joiner
(318) 247-6941, ext 231

Northeast Louisiana University
University Relations
700 University Ave
Monroe, LA 71209

Dr. Alex John
(318) 342-2055

Massachusetts

The NETWORK, Inc
290 S Main St
Andover, MA 01810

Leslie F. Hergert
(617) 470-1080

Michigan

University of Michigan—Ann
    Arbor
School of Education
1036-54 School of Education Bldg
Ann Arbor, MI 48109

Dr. Charles D. Moody
(313) 763-9910

Wayne State University
5050 Cass Ave
Detroit, MI 48202

Trevor Gardner
(313) 577-0920

Minnesota

College of St Thomas
2115 Summit Ave
St Paul, MN 55116

Walter L. Jones
(612) 647-5258

Mississippi

Jackson State University
Department of Continuing
    Education
1325 Lynch St
Jackson, MS 39217

Anita H. Hall
(601) 968-2024

Mississippi State University
Continuing Education
Drawer NX
Mississippi State, MS 39762

Norvel L. Burkett
(602) 325-3473

Missouri

University of Missouri
Midwest Community Education
    Development Center
8001 Natural Bridge Rd
St Louis, MO 63121

Everette Nance
(314) 553-5746

Montana

S.E.E. Institute
Rocky Mountain College

1500 Poly Dr
Billings, MT 59102

Jenny Redfern
(406) 245-6156, ext 214

New Jersey

Consortium for Educational
    Equity
Rutgers University—New
    Brunswick
Federation Hall—Douglass
    Campus
New Brunswick, NJ 08903

Rebecca L. Lubetkin
(201) 932-9808

New Mexico

University of New Mexico
College of Education
Albuquerque, NM 87131

Ernest Gurule
MEC
(505) 277-5706

Norma Milanovich
Department of Secondary/
    Adult Teacher Education
(505) 277-2411

New York

Institute for Urban & Minority
    Education
Columbia University—Teachers
    College
525 W 120th St
New York, NY 10027

Marguerite Ross Barnett
Herminio Martinez
(212) 678-3785

New York University
Education, Health, Nursing &
    Arts Profession School
Washington Square Center
New York, NY 10003

Lamar Miller
(212) 598-2931

North Carolina

University of North Carolina—
    Chapel Hill
School of Education
Peabody Hall 037-A
Chapel Hill, NC 27514

Valora Washington
(919) 966-4449

North Dakota

North Dakota State University
Division of Continuing Studies
State University Station,
Box 5595
Fargo, ND 58105

Sharon Beckstrom
(701) 237-7016

Ohio

Ohio State University Research
    Foundation
1200 Chambers Rd, Rm 106
Columbus, OH 43212

William W. Wayson
(614) 422-1659

Research and Sponsored Programs
Kent State University
301 Wright Hall
Kent, OH 44242

B. Turner
(216) 672-2828

Oklahoma

SW Center for Human Relations
    Studies
University of Oklahoma
555 Constitution
Norman, OK 73037

Ira Eyster
(405) 325-3806

University of Tulsa
College of Education
600 S College Ave
Tulsa, OK 74104

Mary Ellis
(918) 592-6000, ext 2335

Oregon

Interface Consultants, Inc
4600 SW Kelly St
Portland, OR 97201

Francisco Garcia
(503) 222-4564

Northwest Regional
    Educational Laboratory
710 SW 2nd Ave
Portland, OR 97204

Al Argon
(503) 248-6805

Dr. Barbara Hutchinson
Multicultural Education
    Division
(503) 248-6800

Portland State University
School of Education
PO Box 751
Portland, OR 97207

Richard Withycombe
(503) 229-4624

Pennsylvania

University of Pittsburgh
Office of Research
1028 Cathedral of Learning
Pittsburgh, PA 15260

Dr. Ogle B. Duff
(412) 624-5865

South Carolina

University of South Carolina
College of Education
Columbia, SC 29208

Johnnie McFadden
(803) 777-7797

Tennessee

University of Tennessee
College of Education
303 Henson Hall
Knoxville, TN 37916

Frederick P. Venditti
(615) 974-6638

Texas

East Texas State University
College of Education
East Texas Station
Commerce, TX 75428

Amado Robledo
(514) 886-5145

Intercultural Development
    Resource Association (IDRA)
5835 Callaghan Rd,
Suite 350
San Antonio, TX 78228

Elena Vergara
Dr. Gloria Zamora
(512) 684-8180

Southwest Texas State University
Department of Education Bldg
San Marcos, TX 78666

Kathleen E. Fite
(514) 245-2575

Stephen F Austin State University
Box 3010A SFA Station
Nacogdoches, TX 75962

Dr. Bennat C. Mullen
(713) 569-5307

Utah

Weber State College
3750 Harrison Blvd
Ogden, UT 84408

Richard F. Thomas
(801) 626-6650

Wisconsin

University of Wisconsin—
   Milwaukee
Ricardo Fernandez
School of Education/Board of
   Regents
PO Box 413, Enderis Hall
Milwaukee, WI 53201
(414) 963-5663

Claire B. Halverson
Center for Urban Community
   Development
929 N 6th St
Milwaukee, WI 53203
(414) 224-4041

Teacher-Training Programs

The following teacher-training programs were verified from information supplied to the editors by the program directors listed. (Abbreviations: LD-Learning Disabled; BD-Behavior Disordered; MR-Mentally Retarded)

	Language(s)	Special Education Area(s)	Degree(s)
Alaska Title VII Bilingual Program Catherine Collier, Director Box 368, University of Alaska Kuskokwim Community College Bethel, AK 99559 (907) 543-2621	Eskimo Yupik	General	Associate Bachelors
Arizona Dr. Herbert Prehm Department of Special Education Arizona State University Tempe, AZ 85281 (602) 965-4756	Spanish	LD BD MR	Masters PhD
California Herbert Grossman Department of Special Education San Jose State University San Jose, CA 95192 (408) 277-2646	Spanish	LD BD MR	Masters
Colorado Dr. Leonard Baca University of Colorado School of Education Boulder, CO 80303 (303) 492-8468	Spanish	LD BD MR (Curriculum Foundations & Instruction with emphasis in Special Education)	PhD

	Language(s)	Special Education Area(s)	Degree(s)
Florida Dr. Marisal Gavilan Department of Special Education Florida International University Tamiami Campus Miami, FL 33199 (305) 554-2000	Spanish	LD BD MR	Masters
Illinois Dr. Rafaela Weffer School of Education DePaul University 2323 N University Ave Chicago, IL 60614 (312) 321-8000	Spanish	LD	Masters
Dr. David Sabatio Department of Special Education School of Education Southern Illinois University Carbondale, IL 62901 (618) 453-2121	Spanish	LD BD MR Speech Pathology	Masters Doctoral
Massachusetts Dr. Maria Brisk Bilingual Education Program Boston University 605 Commonwealth Ave Boston, MA 02215 (617) 353-2000	Spanish Chinese French Italian Portuguese	LD BD MR Hearing Impaired	Masters Doctoral
Maria I. Ruiz, Director Bilingual Multicultural Special Education Project Division of Special Education Department of Education Commonwealth of Massachusetts Quincy Center Plaza Hancock St Quincy, MA 02169 (617) 471-0100	Spanish Chinese Greek Haitian Italian Portuguese	Generic Special Education	Masters Inservice training program

	Language(s)	Special Education Area(s)	Degree(s)

Laurie Schloff, Director Silvia Martinez,
   Bilingual Speech-Language
   Pathologist
Department of Speech
   Pathology & Audiology
Northeastern University
360 Huntington Ave
Boston, MA 02115
(617) 437-2200
	Spanish
	Chinese
	French
	Italian
	Vietnamese
	Portuguese
		Speech Pathology	Masters

Sister Loretto Hegarty Regis College Weston, MA 02193 (617) 893-1820	Spanish Chinese French Italian Vietnamese Portuguese Japanese Haitian	Generic Special Education (Mildly Handicapped) Moderate Special Needs Educator Applied Psycholinguistics	Masters & License Masters & License Masters
New Jersey Mihri Napoliello Kean College of New Jersey Morris Ave Union, NJ 07083 (201) 527-2195	Spanish	Generic	Masters

New Mexico
 	
Dr. Eloy Gonzales Department of Special Education
University of New Mexico
Albuquerque, NM 87131
(505) 277-5019
	Spanish	LD
		MR
		Diagnosis
		Minority Child
			Masters PhD in
			   Special
			   Education

New York
 	
Carmen Dinos Bilingual Program
School of Education
Brooklyn College
2201 James Hall, Bedford Ave
   & Ave H
Brooklyn, NY 11210
(212) 780-5953
	Spanish
	French
	Chinese
		LD
		Gifted
		[Both are under
		   consideration]
			Bachelors Masters

	Language(s)	Special Education Area(s)	Degree(s)
Dr. John Hicks Department of Special Education Fordham University at Lincoln Center 113 W 60th St New York, NY 10023 (212) 841-5100	Spanish	LD BD MR	Masters

Lexington School for the Deaf
LISTO (Latino Inservice
  Training & Orientation
  Project)
30th Ave & 75th St
Jackson Heights, NY 11370
(212) 899-8800
	Spanish/
	English
		Hearing
		Impaired
			*Inservice
			project

Janet Finell Department of Guidance & Counseling Long Island University Brooklyn Center Brooklyn, NY 11201 (212) 834-6000	Spanish	Mainstreaming	†Nondegree
Basilio Serranio Bilingual Teacher Education Program College of Education SUNY, Old Westbury Old Westbury, NY 11568 (516) 876-3332	Spanish	Generic	Bachelors

*Train school personnel to work with Hispanic hearing impaired.

†Inservice training for regular educators (nonspecial education) working with mainstreamed handicapped youngsters.

Bilingual/Bicultural Special Education Training Projects*

PREPARATION OF TEACHERS OF BILINGUAL/ MULTICULTURAL HANDICAPPED (ARIZONA)

This project's primary goal is to assist the Department of Special Education at Arizona State University in developing a masters degree program which will prepare special education teachers to provide educational services to handicapped bilingual/multicultural children. The training focus is on service to mentally retarded, language disordered, and behavior disordered children in Arizona and the surrounding Southwest region.

The instructional staff consists of three bilingual/bicultural persons, as well as other faculty members within the Department of Special Education. Training activities include course work and practicum experience.

Trainee assessments are based on academic performance and the demonstration of designated competencies during the practicum experience. An evaluation of the project's impact on the children served is obtained from reports made by classroom teachers, school administrators, parents, and community services personnel.

The instructional resources used for training are largely developed in-house; however, some diagnostic and instructional strategies are modified and adopted from outside sources. The information dissemination process is currently being organized by project staff. It is anticipated that this task will be completed within one year of the project's implementation.

---

*Reprinted from Patricia Landurand, et al. *Bridging the Gap between Bilingual and Special Education,* Pages 19–34. Reston, VA: ERIC Clearinghouse on Handicapped and Gifted Children, 1980. These projects were funded in fiscal year 1979 by the Bureau of Education for the Handicapped/Division of Personnel Preparations.

Editors' Note: Users of this book interested in the current status of a specific program should call or write the individuals listed after each description.

For further information, contact: Alfonso Prieto, Robert Rueda, PhD, Department of Special Education, Arizona State University, Tempe, AZ 85281 (602) 965-4756.

MULTICULTURAL/SPECIAL EDUCATION PROGRAM DEVELOPMENT (CALIFORNIA)

The inservicing of faculty will involve apprising regular educators of various social and educational issues affecting bilingual/bicultural handicapped children. The project serves the full spectrum of handicapped children in San Diego county and the southeast region of California.

The incorporation of a preservice component into the regular educational coursework of the Multicultural, Elementary, Secondary, and Counselor Education Departments (San Diego State University) is a current concern. Thus, those individuals now receiving training in these departments will be provided with a framework for effective management of mainstreamed special education children and youth.

The instructional staff consists of two bilingual persons, as well as other faculty members within the Department of Multicultural Education. Most training resources and materials are being developed in-house; however, some materials from outside sources are being modified and subsequently adopted.

Project staff and trainees are currently developing assessment techniques to be used in the collection of trainee and child change data.

For further information, contact: Dr. Viola Sierra, Department of Special Education, San Diego State University, 5300 Campanile Dr, San Diego, CA 92182 (714) 265-5931/6665.

BILINGUAL CROSS CULTURAL SPECIAL EDUCATION TRAINING (CALIFORNIA)

This project provides preservice training to Spanish speaking graduate level students. Training offers participants the opportunity to earn a masters degree in Special Education and specialization credentials in the areas of learning, handicapped, and communicative disorders. Project efforts directly serve bilingual/bicultural handicapped children and youth in the midregion of California. Collaborative arrangements have been made with local education agencies for service delivery.

There are 31 trainees and two bilingual and seven nonbilingual staff persons involved in the project. Procedures for determining project impact on trainees and the target population are currently being developed. While many of the instructional materials have been developed by project staff, some materials from other sources have been modified and subsequently adopted.

For further information, contact: Dr. Gilbert Guerin, Department of Special Education, Washington Center, San Jose State University, San Jose, CA 95192 (408) 277-2646.

BILINGUAL INSTRUCTORS FOR THE HANDICAPPED CHILDREN (BIHC) TRAINING PROGRAM (CALIFORNIA)

The objective of this inservice program is to train Asian bilingual teachers in educating handicapped children. Upon completion of the program, the students can earn an MA and specialist credentials. The project serves northern California and the San Francisco Bay area.

Presently, there are 20 trainees and 24 instructors, 19 of whom are bilingual. Most of the resource materials used in the project were designed by students and faculty. Training activities consist of seminars, written assignments, review of concept media (e.g., films, videocassettes, and slide tapes), and a practicum experience.

Participants are evaluated by semester exams and teacher observations of performance practica. The Evaluation Institute at the University of San Francisco is responsible for follow-up surveys of trainees' employability and for determining project impact.

The project operates in collaboration with the University of San Francisco faculty and administration, Bilingual Education organizations (Bay Area Bilingual Educational League, Inc, California Association for Asian Bilingual Education, and the BELI Clinic), and several school districts' handicapped education programs.

For further information, contact: Dr. Leo P. K. Yam, Rossi Wing, Lone Mountain, University of San Francisco, San Francisco, CA 94117 (415) 666-6876/8.

BILINGUAL HISPANIC COMMUNICATIVELY HANDICAPPED CHILDREN (COLORADO)

The goal of the project is to develop a model program to train masters and doctoral level students as speech/language pathologists who provide services to bilingual/bicultural communicatively handicapped persons. The project serves all bilingual disabilities except the visually handicapped. The geographic location most directly served is metropolitan Denver with outreach to rural Colorado. There are currently six MA students and three PhD candidates enrolled in the project.

Learning activities being designed include a curriculum of courses and a practicum. An assessment of trainee competencies is determined by "project specific" clinician evaluation forms and the "ABC Method of Analysis." Participant midterm and final practicum reports provide valuable information about project effectiveness with respect to influencing changes in a child's behavior.

Three university professors in the Communication Disorders and Speech Science Division are actively involved in the project. While none of these instructors is bilingual, seven bilingual individuals on the nine member Advisory Council will help design the model program.

For further information, contact: Patricia Hale Killian, PhD, Communication Disorders and Speech Science, University of Colorado, MA 108, Box 88, Denver, CO 80240 (303) 629-2538 or Natalie Hedberg Daves, PhD, Communication Disorders and Speech Science, University of Colorado, MA 108, Box 88, Denver, CO 80240 (303) 629-2479.

LEARNING DISABILITIES PROGRAM FOR TEACHERS OF NON-ENGLISH SPEAKING CHILDREN (ILLINOIS)

This three-year preservice project is designed to train bilingual specialists in learning disabilities (MA or MEd) to meet the educational needs of non-English speaking children. The instructional staff during the academic year includes one bilingual and two monolingual professors.

The training includes: (1) theoretical and practical experiences in the course work; (2) practical experiences with parents to provide information for their understanding of the educational and emotional needs of their children; and (3) collection of longitudinal data to document child change data and to analyze the effectiveness of instruments, including nondiscriminatory testing.

The collection of trainee-change data is accomplished through the use of "project specific" questionnaires and academic and practicum course work peformance.

The geographic locations served by the project are the Chicago Metropolitan area and adjacent suburbs. A working relationship for referrals has been established with El Hogar del Nino (a day care center).

For further information, contact: Rafaela E. Weffer, PhD, School of Education, DePaul University, 802 W Belden, Chicago, IL 60614 (312) 321-8390/1.

MINORITY ISSUES INSERVICE PROGRAM (MIIP) (KANSAS)

This three-year cooperative project, sponsored by the University of Kansas and the Kansas City, Missouri School District, provides inservice training to local regular education teachers and special education personnel employed in 20 area elementary schools. Special emphasis is on increasing the knowledge and skills of these practitioners who will, in turn, serve handicapped and multicultural children in the Kansas City, Missouri School District.

A package is currently being developed for training purposes. It includes: a training guide and manual for principals and/or special education leaders; an inservice training monograph for teachers; and a 15-minute filmstrip cassette kit. Trainers will be evaluated by pre- and posttests, a survey questionnaire, and a mastery exam.

Project information is disseminated throughout the local school district and nationally through The Council for Exceptional Children.

For further information, contact: Dorothy Preston, Program Implementation Specialist, The University of Kansas Medical Center, College of Health Sciences and Hospital, Rainbow Blvd at 39th St, Kansas City, KS 66103 (913) 588-4526.

TRAINING PROGRAM FOR SPEECH LANGUAGE PATHOLOGISTS AND TEACHERS TO WORK WITH MINORITY/ BILINGUAL PRE SCHOOL AND PRIMARY GRADE CHILDREN (MASSACHUSETTS)

This project offers preservice training for graduate students (MA) in speech and language pathology. The project primarily serves the communicatively disordered in Boston and, in particular, those living in the Roxbury and Dorchester communities.

A collaborative instructional arrangement with Northeastern University allows selection of four or five graduate students each quarter to participate in the project. Thus, trainees can benefit from a practicum experience in addition to University academia.

Trainee evaluations are based on academic performance, as well as performance during the practicum. Assessment focuses on diagnostic competency; quality of interaction with clients; preparation for therapy, personal, and professional behaviors; and other specialized skills. Child change data are collected mostly through protocols designed to provide diagnostic information on speech and language impairment.

The instructional staff includes one bilingual speech pathologist with consultancy assistance from instructors in the Speech and Pathology Department at Northeastern University and from professionals in the Massachusetts educational community.

For further information, contact: Elise S. Kaufman, MS, Department of Audiology and Speech Pathology, College of Education, Northeastern University, 360 Huntington Ave, 106 Forsyth, Boston, MA 02122 (617) 437-2495.

BILINGUAL SPECIAL EDUCATION PROJECT (BISEP) (MASSACHUSETTS)

This project developed from the collaborative efforts of the Massachusetts Advisory Council of Bilingual Education to the Department of Education and the Bilingual Special Education Training Group Task Force within the Division of Special Education's Manpower. The project serves the full spectrum of handicapped minority children and youth in Massachusetts.

Project BISEP conducted a comprehensive assessment of student needs to determine the nature of the particular services required. The project has made extensive efforts to address these needs through developing publications and holding conferences on nondiscriminatory assessment; conducting regional workshops for school personnel at local, regional, state, and national levels on issues in bilingual/bicultural special education; and delivering statewide inservice training to speech therapists and psychologists in assessing limited English proficiency students. Inservice training is designed to help teachers screen students for language proficiency and special needs. Another focus is the assessment of the learning styles and the problems of limited English speaking children.

Since September 1979, BISEP has initiated and funded two model bilingual/bicultural special education graduate programs. One is housed at Regis College; the second is at Fitchburg State College, with a site at Westfield State College—all in Massachusetts. At present, 50 certified bilingual/bicultural teachers are enrolled in the licensure program.

In addition to the above efforts, BISEP operates an information dissemination service. The project team responds to individual requests for information regarding child placements, programs, and resources available for limited English proficiency students.

Present BISEP activities include: the updating of research and program models in bilingual/bicultural special education; the delivery of local and regional inservice training; proposal writing for additional funding; and the delivery of daily technical assistance to school systems, agencies, and parents in the area of linguistic minorities and special education.

For further information, contact: Patricia Landurand, Regis College, Weston, MA 02193 (617) 893-1820.

REGULAR EDUCATION INSERVICE: GENERIC SPECIAL TEACHER TRAINING PROGRAM (ELEMENTARY, SECONDARY, BILINGUAL) (MASSACHUSETTS)

Preservice training involves course work, research projects, seminars, and practicum experience. Upon completion of project activities, participants earn a masters degree. While the immediate concern of the project is to train qualified generic special teachers, these trainees are expected to collaborate with and give ongoing support to regular classroom teachers. The project services the full spectrum of handicapped children in Boston and Chelsea, Massachusetts.

Specific project goals are: (1) to develop a model Bilingual/Generic Special Teacher Training Program that will bridge the gap between bilingual and special education, first at the elementary level and later at the secondary level; (2) to equip bilingual teachers with special education competencies; (3) to provide needed resources for alternative instructional materials and strategies; and (4) to make parents and community liaison personnel aware of their relationship to the total system of services.

At present, there are 12 bilingual trainees, 8 bilingual instructors, and 20 nonbilingual instructional staff. Trainee change data are obtained through an analysis of pre- and posttests and practica experience reports. Further assessment of project impact, with respect to the target population, is determined through practica statistics.

For further information, contact: Sr. Loretto Hegarty, PhD, Regis College, Graduate Division, 235 Wellesley St, Weston, MA 02193 (617) 893-1820, ext 240.

SCHOOL PSYCHOLOGISTS TRAINING ON NONDISCRIMINATORY ASSESSMENT OF CHILDREN WHO HAVE SPECIAL NEEDS AND LIMITED ENGLISH SPEAKING ABILITY (MASSACHUSETTS)

The primary goal of the project is to develop and implement a program to train practicing school psychologists in nondiscriminatory assessment/ evaluation of bilingual and Limited English Speaking Ability (LESA) children with special needs. The project also provides participants with information about resources available within the school and community.

The 36 trainees enrolled in the project serve LESA children with special needs in Boston and the northeastern region of Massachusetts. The resources and materials used in project implementation were largely developed by project staff. There are eight bilingual and two nonbilingual staff persons assigned to this project.

As assessment of trainee progress is based upon the demonstration of designated competencies. An examination of the kinds of services being delivered by trainees within the school and community is another indicator of project impact.

Information dissemination activities include local presentations about project operations and workshops at state and national conferences.

For further information, contact: Diane Coulopoulos, PhD, Psychology Department, Simmons College, 300 The Fenway, Boston, MA 02115 (617) 738-2172.

MAINSTREAMING INSERVICE PROJECT FOR CHILDREN OF LIMITED ENGLISH SPEAKING ABILITY (NEW JERSEY)

Inservice training is designed to expand the bilingual/bicultural awareness of resource teachers and child study team members and to enhance the instructional competencies of bilingual/bicultural education teachers in dealing with handicapped LESA students. The project focuses on meeting the needs of all handicapped children in Union and Essex Counties in New Jersey. Collaborative arrangements have been made with the local education agency, the New Jersey bilingual teachers, and the local task force on Bilingual Special Education.

There are 42 trainees and five bilingual and two nonbilingual instructional staff persons on the project. Impact on the trainees is determined through an analysis of pre- and posttests and attitude scales. Project staff are currently developing an instrument to be used in the collection of child change data. Another project goal is to produce a bilingual manual (including a Spanish-English glossary) to be used by special education personnel.

For further information, contact: Ana Maria Schuhmann, School of Education, Kean College of New Jersey, Morris Ave, Union, NJ 07087 (201) 527-2405.

RECRUITMENT AND TRAINING OF BILINGUAL/BICULTURAL STUDENTS (COMPONENT 8) (NEW MEXICO)

This project is designed to provide training for bilingual/bicultural special education teachers interested in intensive preparation in one of four concentrations: learning disabilities, mental retardation, behavior disorders, or giftedness. There are five masters degree students and one doctoral candidate currently enrolled. Participants are recruited from Arizona, Colorado, New Mexico, and Texas. They must indicate a desire to return to their communities after training and also must hold a bachelors degree in Bilingual Education.

In addition to earning their respective degrees, trainees have the opportunity to increase their language proficiency in either Spanish or a Native American language. They are also prepared to serve as resource links in the communication network between the Special Education Department and bilingual/bicultural special education programs across the state and in the southwest region.

The instructional staff consists of two bilingual/bicultural persons and the 13 faculty members in the Department of Special Education. Procedures for determining project impact on the trainees and the target population are currently being developed under the combined efforts of staff and participants.

For further information, contact: Dr. Eloy Gonzalez, Department of Special Education, College of Education, University of New Mexico, Albuquerque, NM 87131 (505) 277-5018.

TRAINEESHIPS IN PRESCHOOL EDUCATION FOR THE HANDICAPPED (NEW MEXICO)

The primary objective of this project is to provide teachers with a set of competencies and/or skills that will prepare them to address the needs of young bilingual/bicultural handicapped children. Upon completion of training, participants earn nine graduate hours which may be applied toward either a masters degree or continuing education units. Although the emphasis of this project is inservice for teachers, some graduate students are involved in the training curriculum.

The project has the capacity to accommodate 28 to 32 inservice trainees. One bilingual and four nonbilingual staff persons are involved with the project. While many training and/or resource materials are being developed by staff, some materials from other sources ar modified and subsequently adopted.

Project efforts most directly serve bilingual/bicultural handicapped children in 32 counties in New Mexico. A brochure explaining project operations is disseminated mostly to elementary school superintendents; directors of special education; early childhood programs in public, private and parochial schools; and all agencies within the state that service the developmentally disabled. Copies of this brochure were distributed at the fall and spring meetings of the New Mexico Council for Exceptional Children in Albuquerque and Roswell.

This training project operates in collaboration with the Department of Special Education, Areas of Bilingual Education, Educational Management and Development, and the Indian Affairs Project.

For further information, contact: Glenna Kyker, Coordinator, Area of Special Education, Department of Education Specialities, University of New Mexico, Box 3 AC, Las Cruces, NM 88003 (505) 646-3237.

PREPARE AND RETRAIN TEACHERS IN ADAPTED PHYSICAL EDUCATION (NEW MEXICO)

This project offers preservice training for graduate students who, upon completion of the project, earn either an MA or PhD degree. The project also has a nondegree/inservice component for retraining teachers in adapted physical education.

Participant training addresses the needs of all handicapping conditions. Project efforts are concentrated in New Mexico and the bordering areas of Colorado, Arizona, and Texas.

At present, there are seven instructional MS students and two PhD candidates involved in the project. Information relative to project effectiveness and to trainee change is obtained through competency demonstrations, checklists for employers, surveys, and questionnaires. Child change data are obtained from reports made by classroom teachers, parents, and community services personnel.

Many of the project's resources have been adapted from: I Can Program—Michigan State University; project EXPLORE (Expanding Programs and Learning in Outdoor Recreation and Education)—Portland State University; PEOPEL (Physical Education Opportunity Program for Exceptional Learners)—Phoenix Unified School District; PREP (Preschool Recreation Enrichment Program)—Maryland National Capital Park and Planning Commission; Project ACTIVE (All Children Totally Involved Exercising); Project PELRA (Physical Education Least Restrictive Alternatives); and STAR (Staff Training for Adapted Recreation).

Dissemination activities include annual project reports, communication with public schools and local/community interest groups, and participation in the National Consortium of Physical Education and Recreation.

The Gallup Branch of the University of New Mexico is in the process of incorporating an AA degree in recreation with a training component in physical education that will be modeled after this project.

For further information, contact: Ernest K. Lange, EdD, Johnson Gymnasium, College of Education, University of New Mexico, Albuquerque, NM 87131 (505) 277-5933.

PROGRAM ASSISTANCE GRANT: GRADUATE PROGRAM IN BILINGUAL SPECIAL EDUCATION (NEW YORK)

The project objective is to increase the number of qualified bilingual/bicultural special education teachers, bilingual diagnosticians, bilingual resource room specialists, and bilingual/early childhood/special educators in the New York City area. This training offers its participants the opportunity to earn a masters degree in Science with a specialization in Bilingual Special Education (Hispanic focus).

Five bilingual and approximately 15 nonbilingual staff persons provide instruction and on site supervision to 28 trainees on various issues relevant to the full spectrum of the bilingual/bicultural handicapped. Collaborative arrangement with a broad cross section of specialists and clients in public and private institutions contribute to project effectiveness.

Trainee and child change data are gathered through a variety of sources: graduate assessment of special education programs; evaluation of on the job graduate performance; assessment of student competencies; and student inventories. Long-term effects of the project may be determined by longitudinal case studies which focus on graduates' professional contributions and employer ratings of job performance.

Information dissemination activities include the preparation of exhibits, discussions, workshops, videotapes, publishable research, and a resource center.

For further information, contact: Carmen D. Ortiz, PhD, Graduate Programs, Bilingual Education Program, Bank Street College of Education, 610 W 112th St, New York, NY 10025 (212) 663-7200, ext 391.

PROJECT MAINSTREAM (NEW YORK)

Project Mainstream operates as a collaborative effort under the auspices of Long Island University—Brooklyn Center, and New York City Community School District No. 13. The project is a nondegree/certificate program. It offers inservice training to 35 educators interested in serving the needs of all mildly handicapped bilingual/bicultural individuals within the Bedford Stuyvesant and Fort Green Communities implemented by educators with an expertise in educating the bilingual/bicultural handicapped child. The instructional process involves the use of lectures, discussions, and multimedia presentations. Trainees participate actively in experiential activities. On site school visits and follow-up seminars are also included. Both trainee change data and child change data are collected through the use of scales and questionnaires. Information regarding project functions is made available primarily in articles and reports.

For further information, contact: Dr. Janet Finell, Guidance and Counseling, Brooklyn Center, Long Island University, Brooklyn, NY 11201 (212) 834-6162.

FORDHAM UNIVERSITY SPECIAL EDUCATION PROGRAM: BILINGUAL/BICULTURAL SPECIAL EDUCATION (NEW YORK)

The Special Education Program at Fordham University is a graduate program offering MS, PhD, and professional diplomas in Educational Psychology with a concentration in Special Education. The project provides training in the full spectrum of handicapping conditions and serves both Manhattan and the Bronx in New York. Most training resources are developed in-house with the cooperation of the Special Education program; however, existing curriculum and diagnostic materials have been modified by project staff and subsequently adapted into project operations.

The project functions as a joint effort of the Special Education Program, the School Pyschology Program, and the Bilingual Education Department within the university. At present, there are 10 MS students and 50 bilingual teachers per year involved in the project. These students and teachers are drawn from the New York City Public School System, particularly District Numbers 3, 4, 7, and 9. Trainee assessments are based on coursework and reports from field supervisors about participant performance and competencies during the practicum. Further evaluation of project impact, with respect to the target population, is determined by classroom teachers' reports.

Information dissemination activities include organizing and implementing a series of workshops and the publication of a locally distributed newsletter.

For further information, contact: Dr. John Hicks, School of Education at Lincoln Center, Fordham University, New York, NY 10023 (212) 841-5276.

NEW PREPARATION FOR EDUCATORS OF HISPANIC HEARING IMPAIRED CHILDREN—LATINO INSERVICE TRAINING AND ORIENTATION PROJECTS (LISTO) (NEW YORK)

The objective of this inservice project is to train educational staff and social service personnel to improve their services to Hispanic hearing impaired children and their families in the areas of bilingual/bicultural education and home/school relationships. In addition to working with the

State Education Departments of Connecticut, Rhode Island, and New York, the project has made collaborative training/activity arrangements with the Rhode Island School for the Deaf and the Bank Street College of Education in New York. The geographic area served by this project is the entire northeastern region of the United States.

LISTO presently accommodates 24 .trainees. An approach to the collection of trainee change data and child change data is currently being developed.

The instructional staff consists of eight people, six of whom are bilingual. The project maintains that "the organization of training precludes the division of staff into bilingual instruction and nonbilingual instruction."

At present, the project is engaged in intensive dissemination activities with the schools or systems involved in the project. A presentation about project operation was made at the National Association for Bilingual Education (NABE) Conference, April 16-24, 1980, in Anaheim, California.

See Dr. Lerman's article, "Improving Services to Hispanic Hearing Impaired Students: Relationship to Bilingual Education" in Chapter One of this document [Patricia Landurand et al. *Bridging the Gap between Bilingual and Special Education*. Reston, VA: ERIC Clearinghouse on Handicapped and Gifted Children, 1980] for an indepth discussion of the LISTO project.

For further information, contact: Dr. Alan Lerman, Training, Research and Educational Evaluation Division, Lexington School for the Deaf, 30th Ave & 75th St, Jackson Heights, NY 11370 (212) 899-8800.

VOLUNTEER INTERPRETERS FOR PARENTS OF HANDICAPPED CHILDREN—BILINGUAL VOLUNTEER PROGRAM (TEXAS)

The primary objective of this project is to train 40 bilingual/bicultural community volunteers to assist families unfamiliar with the English language in locating community support and services for their handicapped children. The training focus is on the preparation of volunteers as interpreters to *all* areas and agencies of special education in order to help educate parents of handicapped children. The project serves the deaf/hard of hearing within the bilingual/bicultural communities in the Houston, Texas area. Project activities emphasize inservice training through practicum experiences in 1 of 15 designated social service agencies. Volunteers serve as interpreters in various health, education, and community social service agencies.

For further information, contact: Marilyn E. Perryman, Adult and Continuing Education, Houston Community College System, 2800 Main St, Suite 405, Houston, TX 77002 (713) 524-2128.

BILINGUAL PROGRAM IN COMMUNICATION PATHOLOGY (TEXAS)

This project offers an MS in Communication Pathology, as well as a nondegree/inservice component and a student recruitment component. Training emphasis is on the communicatively impaired in bilingual (primarily Hispanic) populations.

Trainees are selected primarily from the state of Texas; however, enrollment is open to any student in the United States, trusts, or territories who is proficient in a language other than English. At present, four masters degree candidates are enrolled in the project. An assessment of participant performance and project effectiveness is addressed by a ''project specific'' discrepancy evaluation model.

The instructional staff consists of one bilingual and seven monolingual (English speaking) individuals. Collaborative arrangements include: (1) field-based clinical placements for students—Ft. Worth Independent School District, Tarrant County Easter Seal Society, Harris Hospital, and the Child Study Center; (2) reciprocal guest lectures by project staff and faculty at Texas Woman's University (Denton), Southern Methodist University (Dallas), and Texas Wesleyan College (Ft. Worth); and (3) the provision of clinical services to communicatively handicapped children in those community agencies that cannot provide these services in Spanish, including small surrounding public school districts, the Ft. Worth Head Start Program, private schools, church groups, and community groups.

Dissemination activities include newspaper publications, newsletters, radio and television coverage, conferences, meetings, and project announcement brochures.

For further information, contact: Joseph W. Helmick, PhD, or Manuela Juarez, MA, Division of Communication Pathology, Miller Speech and Hearing Clinic, Texas Christian University, Fort Worth, TX 76129 (817) 921-7620.

BILINGUAL SPECIAL EDUCATION PROGRAM (TEXAS)

This project provides preservice training in the areas of evaluation, diagnosis, and counseling. Upon completion of project activities, participants will earn an MS in Education with specialization credentials as either an educational diagnostician, diagnostic resource teacher, or special education counselor.

Participant training addresses the needs of all handicapped children and youth but places particular emphasis on learning disabilities. Currently, there are eight trainees. The instructional staff is comprised of two bilingual and 18 nonbilingual persons.

Learning activities include a curriculum of coursework and practical experience. While many of the instructional resources have been developed by project staff, some commercial diagnostic instruments are used. In addition, some materials are modified and subsequently adopted from other sources. Assessment of trainee competencies is determined by means of "project specific" checklists and field experience performance ratings.

This project most directly serves the bilingual/bicultural handicapped in Houston/Galveston and the Texas Gulf Coast. A collaborative arrangement has been made with local education agencies for service delivery.

For further information, contact: Dr. John L. Carter, School of Professional Education, University of Houston at Clear Lake City, 2700 Bay Area Blvd, Houston, TX 77058 (713) 488-9274.

Networks

NATIONAL DIFFUSION NETWORK

In 1974, the United States Office of Education established the National Diffusion Network (NDN) to promote the dissemination of exemplary educational programs and materials. The network is charged with two main functions: (1) to maintain a national system for delivering information about an increasing variety of successful projects to meet the needs of local school systems; and (2) to ensure that successful projects developed in one state are made available for consideration in all states.

The network is made up of educators who have developed innovative programs which have gained approval for dissemination from NDN's Joint Dissemination Review Panel. Since 1974, 58 programs in the area of the handicapped have been approved, many of these appropriate for use in a bilingual special education setting.

For information about the network and/or locating the facilitator in a particular state, contact: National Diffusion Network Division, Rm 802, Rivera Boulevard, 1832 M St, NW, Washington, DC 20036. Also, request a copy of the latest edition of *Educational Programs that Work,* a listing of all programs selected by the Joint Dissemination Review Panel.

BILINGUAL SPECIAL EDUCATORS NETWORK

The National Association for Bilingual Education (NABE) Special Education Special Interest Group is in the process of developing a computerized network "to collect information about professionals involved in current research in special education for limited-English proficient students; to collect information about professionals implementing training programs to prepare bilingual special educators for their field; and to collect information about professionals implementing programs for bilingual special needs students by area of exceptionality, age, language, and region of the country." Nancy Dew of the Illinois Resource Center is coordinator of program development and the databank. For information about the network, contact: Nancy Dew, Illinois Resource Center for Exceptional Bilingual Children, 500 S Dwyer Ave, Arlington Heights, IL 60005 (312) 870-4143.

Indexes, Databases, Journals, and Newsletters

INDEXES AND DATABASES

*+ Comprehensive Dissertation Abstracts
    Xerox University Microfilms, Ann Arbor, MI 48106.

Current Index to Journals in Education (CIJE)
    The Oryx Press, 2214 N Central Ave, Phoenix, AZ 85004. Monthly.

DSH Abstracts
    DSH Abstracts, American Speech-Language-Hearing Association, 1081 Rockville Pike, Rockville, MD 20852. Quarterly.

Education Index
    H. W. Wilson Company, 950 University Ave, Bronx, NY 10452. Monthly (except July and August).

Educational Administration Abstracts
    University Council for Educational Administration, 29 W Woodruff Ave, Columbus, OH 43210. 3/yr.

*+ Educational Resources Information Center (ERIC)
    National Institute of Education, Washington, DC 20208 and ERIC Processing and Reference Facility, Bethesda, MD.

*+ Exceptional Child Education Resources (ECER)
    The Council for Exceptional Children, 1920 Association Dr, Reston, VA 22091. Quarterly.

*+ Language and Language Behavior Abstracts (LLBA)
    Language and Language Behavior Abstracts, PO Box 22206, San Diego, CA 92122. 5/yr (one issue includes a cumulative index).

 + National Clearinghouse for Bilingual Education (NCBE)
    National Clearinghouse for Bilingual Education, 1300 Wilson Blvd, Suite 132-11, Rosslyn, VA 22209 (800) 336-4560.

---

*Database file available through DIALOG Information Retrieval Service.
+Database file available through Bibliographic Retrieval Systems (BRS).

*+ Psychological Abstracts
> American Psychological Association, 1200 17th St, NW, Washington, 20036. Monthly.

Resources in Education (RIE)
> Superintendent of Documents, US Government Printing Office, Washington, DC 20402. Monthly.

* Special Education Materials (Formerly NICSEM/NIMIS)
> University of Southern California, University Park, Los Angeles, CA 90007.

JOURNALS AND NEWSLETTERS

American Annals of the Deaf
> Conference of Executives of American Schools for the Deaf, 5034 Wisconsin Ave, NW, Washington, DC 20016. 6/yr.

Bilingual Journal
> Evaluation, Dissemination and Assessment Center (EDAC), Lesley College, 49 Washington Ave, Cambridge, MA 02140. Quarterly.

Bilingual Resources
> National Dissemination and Assessment Center, California State University, Los Angeles, 5151 State University Dr, Los Angeles, CA 90032. 3/yr.

Education Unlimited
> Educational Resources Center, 1834 Meetinghouse Rd, Boothwyn, PA 19061. 6/yr.

Exceptional Children
> The Council for Exceptional Children (CEC), 1920 Association Dr, Reston, VA 22091. 8/yr.

Exceptional Teacher
> Special Press, PO Box 2524, Columbus, OH 43216. Monthly.

Hispanic Deaf Newsletter
> Hearing Impairment Program, Department of Special Education, University of Nebraska—Omaha, Omaha, NE 68182. Monthly.

The Journal for Special Educators
> American Association of Special Educators, 179 Sierra Vista Ln, Valley Cottage, NY 10989. 3/yr.

Journal of Learning Disabilities
> Journal of Learning Disabilities, 101 E Ontario, Chicago, IL 60611. 10/yr.

---

*Database file available through DIALOG Information Retrieval Service.
+Database file available though Bibliographic Retrieval Systems (BRS).

Journal of School Psychology
> Human Sciences Press, 72 Fifth Ave, New York, NY 10011.
> Quarterly.

Journal of Special Education
> Grune & Stratton, Inc, Subscription Department, 111 Fifth Ave, New
> York, NY 10003. Quarterly.

Language, Speech, and Hearing Services in Schools
> American Speech-Language-Hearing Association, 10801 Rockville
> Pike, Rockville, MD 20852. Quarterly.

Psychology in the Schools
> Clinical Psychology Publishing Co, 4 Conant Square, Bradon, VT
> 05733. Quarterly.

Teaching Exceptional Children
> The Council for Exceptional Children (CEC), 1920 Association Dr,
> Reston, VA 22091. Quarterly.

The Volta Review
> Alexander Graham Bell Association for the Deaf, 3417 Volta Pl, NW,
> Washington, DC 20007. Monthly.

Directory of Persons

Individuals listed in this section submitted responses to a questionnaire sent to them by the editors. The information provided includes address, telephone number, publications, activities, and any additional comments the respondents wished to share. Users of this section are encouraged to contact the individuals if additional information concerning their availability and/or resource materials is desired.

Robert E. Abbott
Supervisor, Special Education Programs and Services
Waukegan Unit Schools
1319 W Washington St
Waukegan, IL 60085 (312) 336-3100, ext 434

Publications: "Exceptional Bilingual LD's—They Are All Around Us"; "Waukegan Early Entry Bilingual Individualized Programming Assessment in Spanish Developmental Kindergarten Program"
Lectures: "Least Restrictive Environment, Where Do Exceptional Bilingual Students Fit In?"; "Early Childhood Education for Exceptional Bilingual Students"; "Programming Issues in Exceptional Bilingual Education"
Workshops: "Exceptional Bilingual Education"; "BIPAS: A Model that Works"; "Options to Educate the Exceptional Bilingual" (variable length)
Consultancy: Models for Exceptional Bilingual Education; Early Childhood Screening, Diagnostic, and Programming Practice
Resource Materials: Guidelines for BIPAS; Bibliographic Materials; Criterion Assessment
Additional Comments: Consultant to many projects/school districts on bilingual education and designer of BIPAS (Bilingual Education Project).

Chuck Acosta
Bilingual Consultant
Los Angeles County Superintendent of Schools
9300 E Imperial Hwy
Downey, CA 90242 (213) 922-6320

Lectures: "High Intensity Spanish Language Training for Special Education Personnel"; "Why the Need for Bilingual Competencies for Assessment Personnel" (1½-2½ hrs)
Consultancy: Same as lecture topics

Additional Comments: Coordinated two summer institutes for psychologists and language/speech specialists and involved in the development of California legislation pertaining to Spanish language/cultural competencies.

Alba N. Ambert

Assistant Professor and Director, Bilingual Special Education Teacher
  Training Program
University of Hartford
College of Education
200 Bloomfield Ave
West Hartford, CT 06117 (203) 243-4621

Publications: Manual for Identification of Limited English Proficiency Children with Special Needs (Boston, MA: Department of Education, 1980)
Lectures: "The Development and Management of Bilingual Special Education Programs"; "Language Development and Language Disorders in Bilingual Populations"; "Assessment of Hispanics: Shifting the Burden"
Workshops: "Identification and Delivery of Services to LEP Children with Special Needs"; "Parental Rights under Special Needs Legislation"; "The Role of the Bilingual Teacher as Child Advocate"; "Issues in Bilingual Special Education"
Consultancy: Guidelines for the Office for Civil Rights on Educational Services to Linguistic Minorities

Oris C. Amos, PhD

Coordinator of Special Education
Wright State University
373 Millett Hall
Dayton, OH 45435 (513) 873-2678

Publications: Teaching in a Multicultural/Pluralistic Society [Resource Module] (WSU Printing Service; ERIC Document, 1981)
Consultancy: Teaching in a Multicultural/Pluralistic Society
Resource Materials: Module available from Dr. Amos
Additional Comments: The resource module and related activities have been used for both preservice and inservice activities.

H. Roberta Arrigo

Coordinator, Bilingual Special Education Teacher Training Program
Hunter College, City University of New York
440 E 26th St, Rm 714
New York, NY 10010 (212) 481-5164

Lectures: "What is a Bilingual Evaluation?"; "Behavior Management Techniques: Home & School"; "Bilingual Educational Evaluation"; "Problems of Adjustment for Bilingual Children in School and at Home"; "Learning Disabilities and the Bilingual Child"; "Cultural Bias and the Puerto Rican Handicapped Child in the Mainland"; "Problems and Issues in Special Education—the

Minority's Question''; ''Evaluating the Language Skills of Bilingual Children'';
''Criterion-Referenced Testing: A Viable Alternative in the Assessment of Bilingual Children''
Workshops: ''Non-discriminatory Testing'' (1½ hrs); ''Bilingual Assessment—A Case Study'' (1½ hrs); ''Early Identification of Learning Problems among Pre-School Bilingual Children'' (2 hrs); ''Helping Children with Learning Difficulties—Parent Workshop'' (2 hrs); ''Assessment Techniques to be Used with Spanish-Speaking Children'' (2 hrs); ''Children's Figure Drawings as Diagnostic Aids: Cultural Considerations'' (2 hrs)
Consultancy: Assessment; Behavior Management; In- & Pre-service Teacher Training; Program Design; Reading; Language; Parents as Partners

Jean E. Bender
Field Coordinator
National Clearinghouse for Bilingual Education
1300 Wilson Blvd, Suite B2-11
Rosslyn, VA 22209 (800) 336-4560

Publications: Manual for Identification of Limited English Proficient Students with Special Education Needs (State Dept of Massachusetts); *Directory of Special Education Programs Serving Limited English Proficient Students*
Lectures: ''Resources and Identification of LEP Students with Special Needs''
Workshops: Same as lecture topic (1½ hrs)
Consultancy: Bilingual Special Education—Resources and Identification of Students; Classroom Modification Techniques
Resource Materials: Consult the current products list from NCBE

Joan Benevento
Associate Professor
Saint John University
Grand Central & Utopia Pkwys
Jamaica, NY 11439 (212) 969-8000, ext 6456

Publications: ''Special Education in Cyprus'' (*Resources in Education,* October 1981)
Consultancy: UNESCO Consultant to Cyprus: January–May 1980

Ernest M. Bernal, PhD
President
Creative Educational Enterprises, Inc
5203 Hedgewood
Austin, TX 78745 (512) 443-5885

Publications: Methods of Identifying Gifted Minority Students (Princeton, NJ: ERIC Clearinghouse on Tests, Measurement, and Evaluation, ETS, 1980); ''The Education of Gifted Chicano Children'' (In *Educational Planning for the Gifted: Overcoming Cultural, Geographic, and Socioeconomic Barriers,* edited by A.Y. Baldwin; G.H. Gear; and L.J. Lucito. Reston, VA: Council for Exceptional Children, 1978); ''The Education of the Culturally Different Gifted'' (In *The*

Gifted and the Talented: Their Education and Development, edited by A.H. Passow. Chicago: University of Chicago Press, 1979)
Lectures: "Screening and Assessing Students of Limited English Proficiency"; "Special Problems and Procedures for Identifying Minority Gifted Students"; "Bilingual Education for Language Minority Gifted Children"
Workshops: Overcoming Language and Cultural Barriers in Special Education Assessment
Consultancy: Program Evaluation and Assessment

Sr. Maria Goretti Biggins
Reading Consultant (PhD Candidate)
Fordham University
1345 Grand Concourse
Bronx, NY 10452 (212) 538-2424

Publications: Easy Steps to Reading Independence, Primary Level; Easy Steps to Reading Independence, Secondary Developmental Level; Vocabulary Enrichment Book, More Words and Ideas; "Is There a Workable Word Decoding System?"; "Simplifying the Decoding Task"; "The Plight of the Functionally Illiterate Bilingual Prison Inmate"
Lectures: "The Problem of the Bilingual Student Learning to Read in the English Language"; "Using Phonics to Teach the Bilingual Child to Read in the English Language"; "Is Mainstreaming a Viable Choice in a Large Classroom?"; "How Do We Motivate the Problem Reader?"
Workshops: Same as lecture topics (1 hr)
Resource Materials: Books listed above are available from Technique Learning Corporation, Freeport, Long Island

Michael P. Brady
Educational Specialist
Special Education Division
Department of Education
Pago Pago, American Samoa 96799 (overseas) 633-0323

Publications: Holo Imua: A Guide for Teachers of the Severely, Multiply Handicapped (Co-authored with M. Apffel; A. Chung-Ming; G. Kishi; Mi Mattison; and R. Rosenberg. Hawaii: DOE, 1978)
Lectures: "PL 94-142 and Pacific Basin Compliance"; "Cross-Cultural Aspects of Special Education"
Workshops: "General Special Education"; "Severely Handicapped"
Resource Materials: "Issues in the Implementation of PL 94-142 in the Pacific Basin Territories" by M. Brady and D. Anderson

John F. Brosnan
Assistant Director of Pupil Services
Holyoke Public Schools
98 Suffolk St
Holyoke, MA 01040-4499 (413) 536-4294

Publications: "A Systems Approach for Ameliorating Possible Prima Facie Denial of Hispanic/Black Students' Rights through Disproportionate Enrollment in Special Education"
Lectures: "Non-Discriminatory Assessment in Special Education"; "The Hispanic Student in Special Education"
Workshops: "Non-discriminatory Assessment" [staff development] (1 hr)
Consultancy: Non-discriminatory Assessment; Program Evaluations

Joseph S. Caldarera
Director of Special Education
Lower Kuskokwim School District
PO Box 305
Bethel, AK 99559 (907) 543-3611, exts 256/257

Publications: "Planning Services for Young Handicapped American Indian and Alaska Native Children" (Co-author. Washington, DC: US Office of Education, 1980)
Consultancy: Special Education Delivery System Development for Rural School Systems Serving Bilingual Native Americans; Practical Linguistic Factors in Assessing Bilingual Students for Special Education Certification; Gifted and Talented Programs for Bilingual Native American School Population
Additional Comments: School psychologist and special education administrator with nine years of field experience in the area of cross cultural assessment and special education program development for Native American students residing in rural Alaska. President of the Alaska Association of Administrators for Special Education. The consultant services noted above center around program development for bilingual Native American students.

Hilda Rojas Carder, PhD
Senior Psychologist
Counseling and Psychological Services (LAUSD)
1555 Norfolk St
Los Angeles, CA 90033 (213) 625-6171 or

178-E Casuda Canyon Dr
Monterey Park, CA 91754 (213) 284-1926

Publications: Resource Manual for Nondiscriminatory Assessment (State Department of Special Education); *A Model for Assessment of the Bilingual Student*
Lectures: "Assessment of the Bilingual Student"; "The Bilingual Student as an Exceptional Student"; "Using Piagetian Tasks to Assess the Bilingual Student"; "LPAD and the Bilingual Student"; "Art Therapy and the Bilingual Student"; "Learning Potential Techniques and the Bilingual Student"
Workshops: Same as lecture topics (variable length)
Consultancy: Clinical Psychology; Marriage, Family, and Child Counseling; Art Therapy; Educational Assessment
Additional Comments: Taught as professor at the University of Guadalajara in the State Department's Second Language Institute Program. Presently in private business and also hold an administrative position with the Los Angeles Unified School District. Conduct workshops and lectures in English and Spanish.

Berttram Chiang
Assistant Professor
University of Wisconsin—Oshkosh
800 Algoma Blvd
Oshkosh, WI 54901 (414) 424-3420
Workshops: "Using Tutoring Approach to Assist Indochinese Students to Learn English"
Additional Comments: Conducted research in "Socialization and Language Acquisition of the Hmong Students in Wisconsin Schools."

Eladio Cisternas
Strategies for Identification and Academic Development of the Gifted/ Talented Bilingual Student
2160 Euclid Ave
Palo Alto, CA 94303 (408) 325-1548
Lectures: Intensive Spanish Seminar for Special Education Personnel
Workshops: Bilingual Math and Science Instruction (1 wk, 15 hrs); "La Ensenanza del Sistema.Metrico" (2 hrs); "Cultural Implication in Teaching Math" (2 hrs); "La ensenanza de les Matematicas como Motivacion vocacional para professiones Tecnicas y Cientificas" (3 hrs)
Consultancy: Will demonstrate model lessons to Math/Science classes in each participating school and will develop Spanish course outline in Math/Science grades 7 through 10 (the course outlines to become a permanent part of the instructional model of the Secondary Spanish Bilingual); Will develop and establish an individualized, bilingual math management system and curriculum materials
Resource Materials: Cultural Implication in the Teaching of Mathematics; El trabajo individual de los alumnos; El Proceso de Ensenanza en la Escuela; Algunas consideraciones Basicas para un desarrolo practico del nino; Desarrollo Social y Educacion

Roberta Cohen
Bilingual Special Needs Teacher and Consultant
Brockton Public Schools
175 Warren Ave
Brockton, MA 02401 (617) 580-7241
Publications: The Brockton Battery: A Special Needs Assessment for Minority Students
Lectures: "Assessment of Bilingual Students (Spanish): Reading Abilities"
Workshops: "Assessment Tools—Formal & Informal"
Consultancy: Teaching Reading to Bilingual Students; Assessment in Native Language (Spanish)
Additional Comments: Currently in the process of standardizing our testing instrument and would like to contact other school systems interested in being included in the norming sample.

Diane Coulopoulos
Associate Professor of Psychology
Project Director, "TEAM" Training for Equal Access for Minorities
Simmons College
300 The Fenway
Boston, MA 02115 (617) 738-2172

Publications: "Current Practices Regarding Assessment of Children with Limited English Speaking Ability" (In *Proceedings: Non-discriminatory Assessment Materials Sharing Conference.* Special Education Manpower Project, Division of Special Education, August 1979, Pub. #11511); "Non-discriminatory Assessment of Minority Ethnic Children: Position Paper" (Massachusetts State Department of Education, August 1979); "Inservice Training of School Psychologists in Non-discriminatory Assessment of Bilingual Children" (ERIC/CAPS. *Resources in Education,* November 1981); *Current Methods and Practices of School Psychologists on the Assessment of Linguistic Minority Children* (Co-authored with G. De George. Massachusetts Department of Education, in press)
Lectures: "Non-discriminatory Assessment of Linguistic Minority Children"; "A Model Program for Training School Psychologists in Non-discriminatory Assessment"; "Childrearing Practices from a Cultural Perspective"
Workshops: Same as lecture topics (variable length)
Consultancy: Technical Assistance in Developing Non-discriminatory Assessment Procedures for School Systems; Individual Psycho-educational Evaluations of Greek Speaking Children; Research in Bilingual Education and Evaluation
Resource Materials: "A Model Program for Inservice Training of School Psychologists in Non-discriminatory Assessment of Bilingual Children"

James M. Crowner
Professor
Department of Special Education
Southern Illinois University
124 Pulliam Hall
Carbondale, IL 62901 (618) 453-2035

Publications: The Illinois Registry of Psychology with Skills in Evaluating Bilingual, Bicultural Handicapped Children (1974); *The Illinois Registry of Personnel Skills in Assessment of Bilingual, Bicultural Students with Unique Language Needs* (1980)
Lectures: "Multicultural Special Education: A Personal Retrospection and an Agenda for the 80's"; "Mexican Cooperative to Serve Spanish Speaking Handicapped Children"; "The Education of Handicapped Bilingual Children"; "Serving the Exceptional Bilingual Child"
Workshops: "Multicultural Special Education" (1 day)
Consultancy: Teacher and Assessment Personnel Competencies in Serving Hispanic Handicapped Children

William B. Cummings, EdD
Director of Curriculum

Fall River Joint Unified School District
PO Box 89
Cassell, CA 96016 (916) 335-4537

Publications: "Cummings Checklist of Characteristics of Gifted and Talented Children" (ERIC Document, ED 187 065, April 1980)
Workshops: "Using Alternative Criteria to Identify Culturally Different/Educationally Disadvantaged Youth" (1 hr)
Consultancy: Same as workshop topic
Additional Comments: The "Cummings Checklist" has proven to be a powerful instrument for identifying Hispanic youth as potentially gifted.

Barbara Day
Principal
South Texas ISD
510 Sugar Rd
Edinburg, TX 78539 (512) 383-1684

Workshops: "The Bilingual Handicapped Child" (1½ hrs)
Consultancy: Vocational Education for Bilingual Handicapped

Nancy Dew
Coordinator
Illinois Resource Center for Exceptional Bilingual Children
500 S Dwyer Ave
Arlington Heights, IL 60005 (312) 870-4143

Publications: Bridging the Gap between Bilingual and Special Education (ERIC Document, 1981); "Designing an Individualized Math Lab Program for the Bilingual LD Student" (Grades 4–9)
Workshops: "Non-discriminatory Assessment of Limited English Proficient (LEP) Exceptional Children"; "Alternative Program Models Designed to Serve LEP Exceptional Students"; "Designing IEP's for LEP Exceptional Children"; "Language Development Program and Language Use Plans for LEP Exceptional Children"; "Classroom Management Techniques and Curriculum Adaptation for LEP Special Needs Students" (5 hrs each)
Consultancy: Assistance to school districts regarding any aspect of program development for their LEP student population by means of school visits (in Illinois), correspondence, or consultation by telephone
Resource Materials: Videotapes for teacher training: (1) "Non-discriminatory Assessment of LEP Exceptional Children" (Susan Durón, Bilingual Program Evaluator, Program Evaluation and Assessment Section, Illinois State Board of Education); (2) "Policy Options for Insuring the Delivery of an Appropriate Education to LEP Handicapped Children" (Leonard Baca, Director, Center for Bilingual/Multicultural Education, Research and Service, University of Colorado—Boulder); (3)"Establishing Communication with LEP Parents: Helping LEP Parents Understand their Advocacy Role and Due Process Rights" (Richard Figueroa, Associate Professor of Education, University of California—Davis); (4)

"Determining a Language Disorder or Delay in a Bilingual Population" (Henriette Langdon, Program Specialist, Morgan Hill Unified School District, Morgan Hill, California); (5) "Establishing a Language Development Program and Language Use Plan" (Alba N. Ambert, Assistant Professor, University of Hartford, College of Education, Hartford); and (6) "Establishing a Conducive Learning Environment for LEP Minority Students" (Alba Ortiz, Project Director, Bilingual Special Education, Department of Special Education, University of Texas—Austin)

Joseph O.P. Diáz

Assistant Professor
Coordinator, Bilingual Education Teacher Training Program, Division of
   Curriculum and Instruction
Pennsylvania State University
176 Chambers Bldg
University Park, PA 16802 (814) 865-6568

Lectures: "The effect of a bilingual instructional mode on the reading ability of Puerto Rican students"; "La migración puertorriqueña a los Estados Unidos como factor de cambio en la educación americana"; and "Home-School Discrepancies and the Puerto Rican Exceptional Child"

Vilma T. Diaz

Project Manager
Office of Bilingual Education
School Board of Broward County Florida
6500 Grifffin Rd
Davie, FL 33314 (305) 765-6901

Workshops: "The Key to Successfully Developing an BIEP" (3 hrs); "Spanish/ Haitian Immersion Institute" (3 hrs); "Translators Guidelines" (2 days); "Nondiscriminatory Assessment for Bilingual Exceptional Student Education (Referral, Diagnosis, Placement)"
Resource Materials: Resource Guide Book for Teachers of Bilingual Emotionally Handicapped Students; Curriculum Guide for Bilingual SLD

Fernando C. Dominguez

ESL Teacher/Counselor
500 Bard Rd
Oxnard, CA 93030 (805) 486-1602

Lectures: "Counseling Chicano Students"
Workshops: "Cultural Awareness" (1 hr); "Cultural Differences" (1 hr)

Jeronimo Dominguez

Director
WESTAR

345 Monmouth Ave
Monmouth, OR 97361 (503) 838-1220, ext 391

Lectures: "Working with Bilingual (Spanish Speaking) Handicapped Children";
"Test Interpretation to Minority Parents (Spanish Speaking)"
Workshops: Same as lecture topics (variable length)
Consultancy: Working with Parents

Dr. Elva Duran

Assistant Professor
University of Texas—El Paso
Department of Educational Psychology and Guidance
College of Education
El Paso, TX 79968 (915) 747-5300

Publications: "Effectiveness of Direct Instruction on Bilingual Education"
(ERIC Document, 1980); "Curriculum Materials for the Hispanic Handicapped"
(ERIC Document, 1980)
Lectures: "Utilizing Direct Instruction with the Handicapped Hispanic Learner"
Consultancy: Bilingual Special Education Reading and Reading for the Handi-
capped Hispanic; Autism
Material Resources: Curriculum Materials for Hispanic and Hispanic Handi-
capped—Reading; Autism—Vocational Training

Dr. Susan Durón

Bilingual Evaluation Specialist
Illinois State Board of Education
188 W Randolph St, Suite 1400
Chicago, IL 60601 (312) 793-3854

Lectures: "Identification of Learning Disabilities in Children from Non-English
Background"; "Language Problems or Learning Problems?"; Evaluating Bilin-
gual Special Education Programs"
Workshops: "Diagnostic Assessment and Remediation of Bilingual Exceptional
Children" (2–4 hrs); "Evaluating the Effectiveness of Service Delivery to Bilin-
gual Exceptional Children" (2–3 hrs); "Non Test Assessment of Limited English
Proficient Exceptional Students" (2–3 hrs)
Consultancy: Workshops; Teacher Training Institutes; Linguistic and Cultural
Sensitivity; Individual Student Assessment Utilizing a Diagnostic on Assessment
Paradigm; Consultation with State and Local Agencies on Designing a Program
Evaluation Design
Resource Materials: Printed packets on bilingual student assessment utilizing a
transdisciplinary approach

David J. Dutcher

Educational Specialist
Bureau of Indian Affairs
9010 Magnolia Ave
Riverside, CA 92503 (714) 351-6318

Publications: "Implementation of PL 94-142 on the Navajo Indian Reservation" (unpublished manuscript)
Lectures: "Assessment of Native American Children"; "Alternative Approaches to Placement Procedures for Native American Children"
Workshops: How to Conduct In-Service Training Sessions (1 hr)
Consultancy: Assessment, Placement, Program Development, and Evaluation of Special Education Programs for Native American children

Clare S. Figler, EdD
Bilingual School Psychologist
Boston Schools
22 Summit Ave
Winthrop, MA 02152 (617) 726-6566

Publications: Puerto Rican Families with and without Handicapped Children; "Nondiscriminatory Assessment: State of the Art"
Consultancy: School Intervention for the Bilingual, Bicultural Child; School Psychology and the Minority Student; Family; Cognitive/language Assessment; Learning Styles

Paul Finkbeiner, PhD
Penni Foley
Consultant
Program Developer
California State Department of Education Special Education Resource
   Network
721 Capitol Mall
Sacramento, CA 95814 (916) 323-4763 or (916) 972-9752

Publications: "A New Focus In Testing: The Language of the Tester" (Co-authored with R. Figueroa. *Exceptional Child,* 1981)
Lectures: "Second Language and Assessment Training"; "In-Service Training for Special Education Personnel Working with LEP Children"
Workshops: "Bilingual IEP's" (3 hrs); "Special Education and Bilingual Education Legislation" (3 hrs); "Bilingualism—Implications for Special Education" (3 hrs)
Consultancy: Bilingual Special Education; Inservice and Preservice Training
Resource Materials: "Resource materials from Second Language and Assessment Training Institutes" (Abstracts of journal articles, handouts, charts, etc.); "Training Materials for Personnel Working with LEP/Handicapped Students"
Additional Comments: Coordinated statewide training programs in Bilingual Special Education for the past 2 years in California and would be willing to assist other states in setting up similar programs.

Joseph E. Fischgrund
Project Director
Projecto Oportunidad/Rhode Island School for the Deaf

Corliss Park
Providence, RI 02908 (401) 277-3525

Publications: "Language Intervention for Hearing Impaired Children from Linguistically and Culturally Diverse Backgrounds" (*Topics in Language Disorders*, vol. 2, no. 3, March 1982); "The Rationale for Bilingual/Bicultural Programming in a School for the Deaf" (Co-authored with Peter Blackwell. In *The Hispanic Deaf*, Gallaudet College Press, 1982)
Lectures: "Meeting the Needs of Hispanic Hearing Impaired Children" (with Dr. Alan Lerman, Project LISTO); "A Bilingual Program for Hearing Impaired Children"
Workshops: "Bilingual Education for the Hearing Impaired"; "Seminars in Language and Linguistics for Educators of the Hearing Impaired"; "Course in Language Development and Curriculum for Scandinavian Teachers of the Hearing Impaired"

Sandra Fradd
Doctoral Candidate
University of Florida
343 Norman Hall
Gainesville, FL 32611 (904) 392-0761

Publications: "Differences in Styles and Expectations: Latin American and North American College Students" (*Exchange*, in press); "Some Considerations for Teaching Reading" (*Florida Reading Quarterly*, in press).
Lectures: "What's Special about Bilingual Special Education?"

Jill C. Gallaher
Project Associate
HCMP Single Portal Intake Project & The Regional Interagency Center
University of Washington
E.E.U. WJ-10
Seattle, WA 98195 (206) 543-4011

Lectures: "Interdisciplinary Teaming for Communication and Language Intervention in the Classroom"; "Collaborative Service Delivery Models between Public Schools and Community Agencies on Behalf of Handicapped Children and Youth and Their Families"
Workshops: "An Interdisciplinary Approach to Communication and Language in the Classroom: Can We Meet the Needs of All Children?" (2–4 hrs); "The Early Childhood Interagency Transition Model" (1–2 hrs)
Consultancy: On site training and technical assistance in the areas of communication and language intervention, behavioral management; Overall educational programming for young handicapped children and their families; Collaborative service delivery model adoptions

Dr. Anne Y. Gallegos
Assistant Professor, Special Education
New Mexico State University

Box 5701
Las Cruces, NM 88003 (505) 646-2447

Publications: "The Exceptional Bilingual Child" (Co-authored with Garner & Rodriguez. In *The Bilingual Journal*. Cambridge, MA: National Assessment and Dissemination Center for Bilingual/Bicultural Education, 1980); "Maximizing Parent Involvement with Bilingual/Bicultural Handicapped Children: Theory and Practice" (*Journal of Professional Studies*. Colorado State University, Spring 1982); "Los Inocentes: Considering the Special Need of the Mexican American Child" (Co-authored with Gallegos & Rodriguez. *Contemporary Education*, Indiana State University, Spring 1982)
Workshops: "Maximizing Parent Involvement with Bilingual/Bicultural Handicapped Children"; "Bilingual Education/Special Education: An Interface"; "Los Inocentes: Considering the Special Needs of the Handicapped Mexican-American Child"; "Inservice Training for Developing Model Programs for Learning Disabled Students"
Additional Comments: Two grants in this area were funded by the Women's Educational Equity Act titled "Developing Non-Biased Career Education Materials for Handicapped and Minority Girls and Boys" in 1980 and 1981.

Dr. Roberto Gallegos
Associate Professor
New Mexico State University
Box 3AC NMSU
Las Cruces, NM 88003 (505) 646-1941

Publications: "Cashing in on Cognates: Teaching Basic Vocabulary to Intellectually Handicapped Bilingual Children" (Co-authored with Roy Rodriguez and Jack Cole. *The Pointer,* Winter 1979); "Bilingual Education: a Vehicle for Bilingualism and Biculturalism" (Co-authored with R. Rodriguez. NMSU Dialogue Series, February 1979. ERIC Document, ED 180 238); "Bilingualism and Biculturalism for the Special Education Classroom" (Co-authored with Rodriguez, Cole, and Stile. *Teacher Education and Special Education*, vol. 2, no. 4, Summer 1979)
Lectures: "Bilingual Bicultural Special Education: An Interface"; "Los Inocentes: Considering the Special Needs of the Handicapped Mexican American Child"
Workshops: Same as lecture topics (variable length)
Consultancy: Role of Culture
Resource Materials: Developed a videotape on the development of cultural content in Special Education instruction

Eugene E. Garcia, PhD
Professor, College of Education
Arizona State University
Tempe, AZ 85287 (602) 965-6429

Publications: "Bilingualism and Language Impairment" (*Journal of Speech and Hearing Disorders,* 1982)

Lectures; ''Language Assessment''; ''Bilingual Acquisition and its Relationship to Language Impairment''
Workshops: Same as lecture topics
Consultancy: Speech and Language Therapy; Testing
Additional Comments: Forthcoming books are: *The Mexican American Child: Language Cognition and Social Development* (University of Arizona Press, 1982); *Bilingualism in Early Childhood* (University of New Mexico Press, 1982).

Eva M. Gavillan
EdD Research Associate
Private Consultant
3420 16th St, NW #405
Washington, DC 20010 (202) 232-1193

Publications: Report to the Rockefeller Foundation: *Assessment Tools Used with Hispanic Children Suspected of Having Handicaps* (Fall 1981); *Preliminary Report on a Project to Examine the Assessment Tools Used with Hispanic Children* (Bibliography), (Fall 1981); *Information on the Hispanic Pupil Special Needs— Where to Find It* (Summer 1980); *Questions and Answers on Bilingual Special Education; An Interdisciplinary Approach to Help Hispanic Handicapped Children*
Lectures: ''Research in Bilingual Special Education (MR, Sp, HI, LD)''
Workshops: ''Pre-Service Training (graduate & undergraduate) in Bilingual Special Education Assessment and Educational Services''
Consultancy: Teacher Training; In-Service Training in Bilingual Special Education; Assessment and Services
Additional Comments: Presentations can be made in English and/or Spanish.

Michael Gilbert
Associate Professor and Director
Bureau of Educational Research and Field Services
University of the Pacific
School of Education
Stockton, CA 95211 (209) 946-2154

Publications: ''The Development of a Working Paper for Improving the Efficiency of the Individualized Education Program''
Workshops: ''Language, Culture, and Technique Development for Assessment Personnel'' (6 wks)
Consultancy: Inservice Training Evaluation of LEP Assessment Personnel

Eloy R. Gonzales
Associate Professor
University of New Mexico
Department of Special Education
Albuquerque, NM 87131 (505) 277-5019

Publications: ''A Cross-Cultural Comparison of the Developmental Items of Five Ethnic Groups in the Southwest'' (*Journal of Personality Assessment,* vol. 46, no.

2, April 1982); 'Issues in the assessment of minorities'' (Co-authored with B.L. Watson and H.L. Swanson. In *Educational and Psychological Assessment of Exceptional Children*. St. Louis: Mosby, 1982); ''Preparation for Teaching the Multicultural Exceptional Child'' (*Teacher Education and Special Education Journal*, vol. 1, no. 4, Summer 1979, pp. 12–18)
Lectures: ''Translating—Norming Existing Tests''; ''Assessment of the Bilingual Headstart Child''; ''Non-discriminatory Testing''; ''A Cross-cultural Examination of the Developmental Items on the Draw-A-Man''; ''The Culturally and Linguistically Different Child: Evaluation and Public Law 94-142''
Workshops: Same as lecture topics (variable length)
Consultancy: Diagnostician Services; Psychological Testing; Special Education Consultant
Resource Materials: Spanish Translation of the WISC-R (Psychological Corporation, 1981); Spanish Translation of the Key Math (American Guidance Incorporated, August 1981); Spanish-English Reference for Educators (Psychological Corporation, 1981)

Mary Ellen S. Greenlee

Assistant Professor of Linguistics
University of Northern Iowa
English Department, TESOL/Linguistics Section
Cedar Falls, IA 50614 (319) 273-2095

Publications: ''Specifying the Needs of a 'Bilingual' Developmentally Disabled Population: Issues & Cases Studies'' (*Bilingual Resources*, 1981); ''Communicative Competence in Spanish/English Developmentally Disabled Persons'' (*Proceedings of CEC Conference on Exceptional Bilingual Child,* 1981)
Lectures: ''Considerations in Language Assessment of the Exceptional Minority Child''; ''Cross-Linguistic Similarities in Acquisition of Phonology and Discourse''
Workshops: ''Assessment: Where Do We Go from Here?''; ''Children's Speech Perception: A State of the Art Review'' (variable length)
Consultancy: Phonological Development and Disorders; Discourse Analysis of Communication by Normal and Developmentally Disabled Persons
Additional Comments: Particular interest in the question of language maintenance among developmentally disabled persons from minority language communities and the sociolinguistic aspects of bilingual language use among such individuals.

Gilbert R. Guerin

Chairperson
San Jose State University
Department of Special Education
San Jose, CA 95192 (408) 277-2646

Publications: ''Informal Assessment in Regular and Special Education'' (In *Assessment of Minority Students,* Mayfield, 1982)
Consultancy: Informal Assessment

Dr. Delina A. Halushka
Dr. Aurora J. Rosello
Dr. Carmen S. Sadek
Directors
Language Communication Institute
3113 Malcolm St
Los Angeles, CA 90034 (213) 474-5605

Publications: Spanish for Special Education; Topics in Special Education (Edition in Spanish)
Lectures: ''Application of the Technical Knowledge in the Language Training of Psychologists and Speech Therapists''; ''A Model Program: Intensive Spanish Language for Bilingual Teachers on Waiver''
Workshops: Language Communication Institute workshops (variable length depending on needs)
Consultancy: Culture; Methodology; Language
Additional Comments: A brochure on the programs and materials from the Language Communication Institute will be sent upon request.

Natalie L. Hedberg
Professor, Communication Disorders
University of Colorado
Campus Box 409
Boulder, CO 80309 (303) 492-6445

Lectures: ''Communication Problems in Bilingual Children: Social, Cognitive and Linguistic Aspects''; ''Language Abilities in Bilingual Children: Are They Delayed, Deficient or Different, and Does It Matter''
Workshops: ''Evaluation of the Bilingual Child: Social, Cognitive and Linguistic Skills'' (2–6 hrs); ''Meaningful Communication: Components of Change'' (2–3 hrs); ''Story Comprehension and Construction'' (2–4 hrs); ''Increasing Opportunities for Commmunication''
Consultancy: Appraisal and direct or consulting intervention approaches for oral and written language problems in bilingual students
Additional Comments: Project director on the BEH funded grant ''Bilingual Hispanic Communicatively Handicapped Children.''

Alan B. Henkin, PhD
Associate Professor
Director, National Center for Materials and Curriculum Development
University of Iowa
College of Education
Iowa City, IA 52240 (319) 353-5400

Lectures: ''Materials Development for Exceptional LEP Children''
Workshops: ''Writing Readable Materials for LEP Children''
Consultancy: Bilingual/ESL Materials Development; Computer-Aided Learning; Transitional Programs for Indochinese Refugee Students in American Schools

Resource Materials: Indochinese Languages; English/Spanish; English Print A/V & CAI Self-Paced, Individualized Materials in Math, Science, Social Studies, and Language Arts. Write to UI care of Dr. Henkin.

Placido Arturo Hoernicke
Associate Professor
Special Education
Eastern Illinois University
Charleston, IL 61920 (217) 581-5315

Lectures: "Linguistic Differences Mental Retardation"; "Cultural Effects on Mental Retardation"
Additional Comments: Currently working on topics in teacher training and multi-cultural understanding.

Patricia Hutinger
Professor and Project Director
Macomb 0-3 Outreach Project
Western Illinois Universtiy
Macomb, IL 61455 (309) 298-1634

Lectures: "Teacher Training for Educators of Exceptional Bilingual Migrant Young Children"
Workshops: Same as lecture topic (3–5 days)
Consultancy: Program Development for Exceptional Bilingual Young Children

Betty Johnson
Coordinator Bilingual Special Education Program
Fitchburg State College and Fitchburg Public Schools
c/o Reingold School
Fitchburg, MA 01420 (617) 345-6992

Publications: Improving Bilingual Program Management: A Handbook for Title VII Directors (Contributor, National Assessment & Dissemination Center, 1980); "The Bilingual Teacher as Diplomat and Cultural Broker" (NABE Conference, 1982)
Lectures: "Cultural Awareness"; "Methods and Materials in Bilingual Special Education"; "Parent Involvement and Program Evaluation"; "Adapting Materials for Bilingual Special Education"
Workshops: Same as lecture topics (variable length)
Additional Comments: Interest in tailoring workshops to the specific needs of the client. Will travel to New Hampshire, Massachusetts, or Connecticut during school year and am available during the summer to travel elsewhere.

Paula Bouchard Johnson
Director, ESEA Title VII Bilingual Program
Franklin Northeast Supervisory Union

Drawer D, Intervale Ave
Richford, VT 05476 (802) 848-3775

Workshops: "La langue ou dialecte—Standard vs. Nonstandard French" (1½ hr)
Consultancy: Bilingual Early Childhood Education
Resource Materials: Curriculum Guide for Teachers; Inventory of Professional and Instructional Books (available from our program)

Manuela Juárez
Coordinator, Bilingual Program in Communication Pathology
Miller Speech & Hearing Clinic
Texas Christian University
Fort Worth, TX 76129 (817) 921-7620

Lectures: "Language Development in Bilingual Populations"; "Assessment & Treatment of Speech-Language Problems in Infants, Children, Adolescents, Adults/Spanish Speakers"; "Identification of Speech-Language Problems in Minority Language Populations"; "Models for IHE Personnel Preparation Program in the Area of Speech-Language Pathology"
Workshops: Same as lecture topics (variable length from 50 min–2 wks)
Consultancy: Communication Disorders; Minority Language Populations
Resource Materials: Willing to share some of the assessment tools/instruments as well as Spanish forms for taking case histories (medical/speech/language).

Eun-Ja-Kim
Associate Professor, Special Education
Northeast Missouri State University
E Normal St
Kirksville, MO 63501 (816) 785-4682

Publications: "Teaching English to the Bilingual Child in the Classroom"
Lectures: "Bilingual/Bicultural Education" (for various disciplines)
Additional Comments: Major responsibility at the Northeast Missouri State University includes teaching courses in Special Education in the area of emotional disturbance and supervising student teachers in this area. Strong interest in "Bilingual Education." Taught English for six years and have a masters degree in linguistics.

Betty Knight
Director, Division of ESOL/Bilingual Programs
Montgomery County Public Schools
850 Hungerford Dr
Rockville, MD 20850 (301) 279-3441

Lectures: "Bilingual Students and Language Disabilities"; "Diagnosing Language Handicaps in Bilingual Students"
Workshops: Same as lecture topics (variable length)
Consultancy: ESOL; Language Disabilities; Diagnosis/Assessment; Teacher Training; Bilingual Assessment—Team Concept

Additional Comments: Willing to share with others interesting projects and research from Montgomery County Public School District.

Glenna T. Kyker
Diagnostician Trainer
New Mexico State University
Box 3AC
Las Cruces, NM 88003 (505) 646-1101

Publications: "Evaluation of Assessment Instruments Used with American Indians"
Lectures: "Non-biased Assessment for American Indian and Hispanic Children"
Workshops: "Suggested Approaches for Eliciting Optimal Results from Culturally Different Children"; "Assessment of Preschool Children for Gifted Programs"
Consultancy: Assessment (Educational Diagnosis); Assessment of Preschool Minority Gifted Children (program in progress)
Additional Comments: Worked on an Indian reservation as a diagnostician for seven years and presently serve as contract diagnostician for schools with large minority populations. The primary emphasis is on relevant administration and interpretation of standardized tests when used with culturally different groups.

Patricia Medeiros Landurand
Project Director
Multicultural Institute for Change
Regis College
235 Wellesley St
Weston, MA 02193 (617) 893-1820

Publications: Bridging the Gap (ERIC publication); *Culturally Responsive Education: Where Are We, Where Are We Going, How Do We Get There?*; *The Multicultural Education Project*
Lectures: "Issues in Special Education for the Culturally/Linguistically Different Child"; "Practical Program Approaches for Bilingual Special Education"; "History and Legal Aspects in Multicultural Special Education"
Workshops: "Designing and Implementing a Culturally Responsive Classroom"; "Cross Cultural Counseling"
Consultancy: For state department personnel in addressing data collection, monitoring, and technical assistance; for administrators in program design and alternative delivery systems; for teachers in designing and implementing multicultural classrooms and in working effectively with minority parents
Resource Materials: Training Modules for Training College Faculty in Multicultural/Multilingual Special Education
Additional Comments: Conducted workshops in this area for the past six years on a local, state, and national level and will be conducting some of this training internationally during 1981–1982.

Henriette W. Langdon
Program Specialist

Morgan Hill Unified School District
PO Box 927
Morgan Hill, CA 95014 (408) 779-8348

Publications: "Assessment and Intervention Strategies for the Bilingual Language Disordered Student" (*Exceptional Children*)
Lectures: "Bilingual Language Development"; "Language Disorders in the Bilingual Child/Youngster"; "Analysis of Instruments Available to Determine Language Proficiency and Performance of the Bilingual Student"
Workshops: Same as lecture topics (variable length)
Consultancy: Language Assessment of Bilingual Students
Additional Comments: Training in Special Education, Speech and Language Pathology. "Quadrilingual" (French, Spanish, Polish, and English).

Dr. Alan Lerman
Director of Training and Research
Lexington School for the Deaf
75st & 30 Ave
Jackson Heights, NY 11370 (212) 899-8800

Publications: Discovering and Meeting the Needs of Hispanic Hearing Impaired Children (1978); "Improving Services to Hispanic Hearing Impaired Children" (In *Issues in Bilingual/Bicultural Special Education*, Washington, DC: Access, Inc, May 1980)
Lectures: "Cultural Issues vs. Mental Health"; "Organization of Appropriate Educational Services"; "Family Issues and the School"
Workshops: "Values Clarification" (3 hrs); "Testing and Evaluation of Hearing Impaired Students and Programs" (1 day)
Consultancy: Mental Health Programming; Inservice Training; Testing and Assessment

Dolores Ventura Levine
School Social Worker
School Board of Broward County
Office of Bilingual Education
6650 Griffin Rd
Davie, FL 33314 (305) 765-6901

Workshops: "The Key to Successfully Developing an BIEP"; "School Social Worker's View of Parental Involvement in the BIEP"
Resource Materials: Resource Guide Book for Teachers of Bilingual Emotionally Handicapped Students; A Bilingual Special Education Handbook for Parents: "Your Child's Right to Special Education" (available in English and Haitian/Creole)

Linda Levy
Case Manager
PO Box 13178
Tucson, AZ 85732 (602) 628-5791

Publications: "Simple Justice: A Case for Mainstreaming the Severely Emotionally Handicapped Bilingual Preschool Child" (1981); "The Eternal Fire: A Case for Supporting Bilingual Education" (1978)
Workshops: Hispanics and Mental Health in the Barrio (2 hrs); Bilingual Education and the Handicapped Child (2 hrs); Dance Therapy and the Bilingual Child; Poetry Therapy and the Bilingual Child (variable lengths)
Consultancy: Bilingual Education; Dance Therapy; Physical/Sexual Abuse of Children; Abuse and the Mentally Retarded Child
Additional Comments: Background with children and adults is diverse—hence interest in numerous aspects of bilingualism and the need for mental health services to offer therapy that can assist clients whose dominant language is Spanish.

Patricia Liebsch
Exceptional Education Teacher, EMR
1515 W. Lapham
Milwaukee, WI 53204   (414) 384-9900

Publications: Major contributor to the *Bilingual Resource Teachers' Handbook* for Milwaukee Public Schools
Additional Comments: Involved in various bilingual projects because of teaching assingment with exceptional bilingual high school students.

Marie Lindahl
Educational Specialist
Division of Special Education
Bureau of Program Audit and Assistance
Massachusetts Department of Education
54 Rindge Ave Ext
Cambridge, MA 02140   (617) 547-7472

Publications: "Equal Educational Opportunity in Special Education: Legal Mandates and Strategies for Planning"
Lectures: "Legal Mandates"; "Monitoring Disproportionate Enrollment of Black and Hispanic Children in Special Education Programs"; "Implementation of Bilingual Special Education Programs"; "Methods and Materials in Bilingual Special Education"; "Alternative Programming and the Least Restrictive Environment"
Workshops: "Bilingual Special Education Child: Who Is Responsible?"; "Minority Students and Special Education"
Consultancy: Legal Mandates; Program Planning Methods and Materials; Evaluation; Teacher Training
Additional Comments: Developed and taught two graduate courses at Regis College: "Contemporary Issues in Bilingual Special Education" and "Methods and Materials in Bilingual Special Education."

Carmela H. Logan, PhD
Assistant Professor

Department of Curriculum and Instruction
Texas Woman's University
Denton, TX 76204 (817) 566-1039

Publications: Caregiving: A Multidisciplinary Approach (Palo Alto, CA: R. & E. Research Associates, 1981); "Mexican-American Parental Attitudes toward School, How They Affect Children's Attitudes and Academic Performance" (*Journal of Texas Association for Bilingual Education,* 1980); "Assessment of Cognitive, Social, and Psychomotor Behavior of Preschool Handicapped Children" (*Evaluation News,* 1979); "Standardized Testing and the Spanish-speaking Minorities" (*Resources in Education,* 1975)
Workshops: "Cognitive Style and the Minority Student" (2 hrs); "Philosophy and Practice of Effective Caregiving" (2 days); "The Linguistically Different Learner" (2 hrs)

Barbara Luetke-Stahlman
Professor in Charge of Hearing Impaired
University of Nebraska—Omaha
Department of Counseling and Special Education
Omaha, NE 68182 (402) 554-2201

Publications: Editor of the "Hispanic Deaf Newsletter"; "Questionnaire Results from Mexican-American Parents of Hearing Impaired Children in the United States" (*American Annals of the Deaf,* 1976); "Assessing Language and/or System Preferences in a Hispanic Deaf Preschooler" (Co-authored with F. Weiner. In *Hispanic Deaf,* edited by G. Delando. Gallaudet Press, 1982); "Rimas para los niños sordos" (In *Hispanic Deaf Monograph,* edited by G. Delgado. Gallaudet Press, 1982)
Lectures: "Assessing Language Proficiency in the Exceptional Learner"; "Oral Bilingual, Manual Bilingual, and Oral/Manual Bimodal Language Acquisition—Similarities and Implications"; "The Language Needs of Hispanic Deaf Children"
Workshops: Same as lecture topics (variable length)
Consultancy: Assessment; Language Acquisition; Language needs in any area of USA or Spanish-speaking countries
Resource Materials: "Rimas para Los niños sordos" (a sampling of Mexican-American nursery rhymes) (in both Spanish and sign orthography, $4.50)
Additional Comments: Interested in receiving manuscripts for publication in a pilot series "Working Papers in Bilingual Special Education."

Eleanor W. Lynch, PhD
Associate Professor
San Diego State University
Department of Special Education
San Diego, CA 92182 (714) 265-6665

Lectures: "Overcoming Barriers to Parental Participation in Their Child's Special Education Program"
Workshops: Same as lecture topic (variable length)

Consultancy: Parent Involvement; Programs for Handicapped Infants and Young Children
Resource Materials: But I've Tried Everything! A Special Educator's Guide for Working with Parents ($2.25)

Archie J. McKinnon
Associate Professor
College of Education
Division of Special Education
N268 Lindquist Ctr
Iowa City, IA 52242 (319) 353-4779

Additional Comments: Presentation at the CEC Bilingual Conference on Exceptional Children was a discussion of a delivery system for off-campus learning. The presentation "A Mobile Instructional Classroom and Distance Learning" is abstracted in the Exceptional Child Education Resources, September 1981. The full paper is available as a paper or on microfiche from ERIC Document Reproduction Service (EDRS).

Carlos G. Manrique
Psychologist
California State University—Long Beach
15110 California Ave
Paramount, CA 90723 (213) 630-3131, ext 214

Publications: "Counseling the Gifted Minority Students" (*Journal of Counseling Psychology*); "Psychological Assessment of Non and Limited English Speaking Handicapped Students" (*Journal of Bilingual Education*)
Lectures: "Counseling Gifted Minority Students"; "Assessment of Non and Limited English Speaking Handicapped Students"; "Cross-Cultural Counseling"
Workshops: Same as lecture topics (variable length)
Consultancy: Assessment; Counseling Gifted and Limited English Speaking Students

Robert L. Marion
Associate Professor
University of Texas
Education Bldg, Rm 408
Austin, TX 78712 (512) 471-4161

Publications: "Issues in the Education of the Bilingual Learning Disabled Child"; "Communicating with Parents of Culturally Diverse Exceptional Children"
Lectures: "Working with Parents"; "Head Start and Early Childhood"
Workshops: "Parent Involvement"; "Working with Parents" (1½ to full day for each)
Consultancy: Evaluation; Special Service (pupil support) Areas

Virginia Matus
Bilingual Advisor for Division of Special Education
Los Angeles Unified School District
450 N Grand Ave, Rm H-104
Los Angeles, CA 90012 (213) 625-6729

Publications: "A Comparison of the Effects of Bilingual and English-Only Programs on the Reading Achievement of Limited English Proficient Learning Handicapped Students" (Dissertation, in progress)
Lectures: "Program Development and Implementation for LEP-Exceptional Children"; "Meeting the Needs of the LEP-Exceptional Children and Their Parents"
Workshops: Same as lecture topics (variable length)
Consultancy: Developing Programs for LEP-Exceptional Children and Their Parents

Mihri Napoliello
Adjunct Instructor
Kean College of New Jersey
Seton Hall University
117 Meadowbrook Rd
Livingston, NJ 07039 (201) 992-4956

Publications: "Mainstreaming Inservice Project for Children of Limited English Speaking Ability" (Co-authored with Schuhmann. ERIC Exceptional Child Education Report, August 1980)
Workshops: "Characteristics of Handicapped Students for Bilingual and ESL Teachers" (1 hr)

Thomas L. Newcomb
Author/Research/Publisher/Educator
Mesopotamia School and Newcomb Publishing
9108 SR 305
Garrettsville, OH 44231 (216) 527-4258

Publications: A variety of books, resources, and articles on Amish & Mennonite Culture; Amish and Mennonite Languages and Education; Bilingual Education with these groups
Lectures: "Bilingual/Multicultural Education with Amish Children"
Workshops: "Designing Bilingual Education for Amish Children" (variable length)
Resource Materials: Please write for catalog

Paul Pattavina, PhD
Project Director/Adjunct Assistant Professor
University of Texas at Dallas
Box 688
Richardson, TX 75080 (214) 690-2088

Publications: "Generic Effective Competencies and the Personal Efficacy Needs of Hispanic Students in Public School" (Co-authored with Ramirez, 1981)
Workshops: "Competencies for Teaching the Bilingual-Disturbed Adolescent" (variable length)
Consultancy: Behavior Disordered Adolescents: Hispanic Background

Rose M. Payán, PhD
Professional Associate
Educational Testing Service
1947 Center St
Berkeley, CA 94704 (415) 849-0950

Publications: The Development and Validation of a Screening Instrument (PICIS) for Assessing Preschool Children with Speech and Language Disorders (Latin Institute)
Lectures: "Nonbiased Assessment"; "Language Assessment"; "Bilingual Special Education Interface"
Workshops: Roll of Speech and Language Specialists with Bilingual/Spanish Speaking Children
Consultancy: Evaluation; Test Development; Program Development and Implementation; Assessment

Mary Lynn Payne, EdD
Psychologist
PO Box 253
Progreso, TX 78579 (512) 565-3060

Lectures: "Treatment of Exceptional Bilingual Students"
Workshops: "Working with Bilingual Children and Their Families: Emotional Problems"
Consultancy: Private consultation business with schools of the Rio Grande Valley and Houston

Maximino Plata
Associate Professor, Special Education
East Texas State University
Commerce, TX 75248 (214) 886-5935

Publications: "Preparing Teachers for Mexican-American Handicapped: The Challenge and the Charge" (*Teacher Education and Special Education*, vol. 2, no. 4, 1979, pp. 21–27); "Bilingual Special Education: A Challenge for the 1980's" (*Catalyst for Change*, vol. 9, no. 3, 1980, pp. 18–21); "Bilingual Special Education: Challenge for the Future" (*Teaching Exceptional Children*, December 1981, in press); "Bilingual Vocational Education: Neutralizing the Language Barrier for Limited or Non-English Speaking Adolescents" (*Exceptional Children*, 1981, in press)
Lectures: Mainstreaming; Assessment; Instruction; Vocational Education
Consultancy: Same as lecture topics

Karen Bittinger Revak
Special Education Resource Teacher
Public Schools
1460 N Pinal Ave
Casa Granda, AZ 85222 (602) 836-2111, ext 51

Lectures: "Bilingual Steps to Literacy Using Topic Charts and Spalding Phonics and Spelling Methods"
Consultancy: French Translation

Barbara G. Rivero
Teacher/Consultant
Jersey City Board of Education
3053 Kennedy Blvd
Jersey City, NJ 07306 (201) 963-6510

Consultancy: Grant Writing for Projects in Bilingual Special Education

Tim Roberts
Assistant Professor
East Texas State University
Department of Special Education
Commerce, TX 75428 (214) 886-5940

Lectures: "Teacher-Training for the Bilingual Handicapped Pupil"

Fred Rodriguez
Assistant Professor
University of Kansas
215 Bailey Hall
Lawrence, KS 66045 (913) 864-4435

Publications: "Mainstreaming a 'Multicultural' Concept into Special Education—Guidelines for Teacher Trainers"
Workshops: "Multicultural Education"
Consultancy: Multicultural/Non-Sexist Education
Resource Materials: "Mainstreaming a 'Multicultural' Concept into Special Education-Guidelines for Teacher Trainers" (free)

Dr. Richard F. Rodriguez
Assistant Professor
Western New Mexico University
College of Education
Silver City, NM 88061 (505) 538-6332

Publications: "Teacher Competencies for Bilingual/Multicultural Exceptional Children"; "Issues in Bilingual/Multicultural Special Education"

Lectures: "Discriminatory Assessment of Minority Children"; "Parent Involvement and Training"; "Identification of the Gifted"
Workshops: "Methods of Teaching Reading to Bilingual Children" (2 hrs)
Consultancy: Teacher Competencies; Assessment Strategies; Program Development

Roy C. Rodriguez

Assistant Professor
College of Education,
Department of Educational Management and Development
Box 3N
New Mexico State University
Las Cruces, NM 88001 (505) 646-1407

Publications: "Cashing in on Cognates: A Method for Teaching Basic Vocabulary to Intellectually Handicapped-Bilingual Children" (Co-authored with R. Gallegos and J. Cole. *The Pointer*, Spring 1979); "Bilingualism and Biculturalism for the Special Education Classroom" (Co-authored with J. Cole, et al. *Special Education and Teacher Education,* Summer 1979); "The Exceptional Bilingual Child" (Co-authored with R. Gallegos and A. Garner. *Bilingual Journal*, Fall 1980)
Lectures: "Bilingual/Bicultural Special Education: An Interface" (with R. Gallegos); "Bilingual-Bicultural Instructional Vehicles: Learning Centers in a Learning Environment" (with R. Gallegos); "Los Inocentes: Considering the Special Needs of the Mexican American Child" (with R. Gallegos and A. Gallegos)
Consultancy: Bilingual Education Teaching Methods and Procedures

Jacqueline B. Rojas

Assistant Director, Marine Education
Institute for Marine and Coastal Studies
University of Southern California
University Park, D.R.B. 296
Los Angeles, CA 90007 (213) 743-8057

Publications: "Los Niños y el Mar (Bilingual)" (In *Proceedings from Presentations at CEC Conference on Bilingual Special Education,* 1981)
Lectures: "New Approach to Bilingual Special Education (Philosophy & Implications)"; "Use of Cross Age Peers in Teaching a Second Language"
Consultancy: Marine Education and Use of Ocean and Water as Vehicle for Learning

Amparo Ross

Bilingual School Psychologist
Dade County Schools
9770 SW 211 St
Miami, FL 33189 (305) 253-8114

Publications: "Evaluating the Non-English Speaking Handicapped. A Resource Manual for the Development and Evaluation of Special Programs for Exceptional Students" (Volume III-B, Florida Diagnostic and Learning Resources System, Bureau of Education for Exceptional Students, Tallahassee, Florida 32301, 1981)
Lectures: "Oral Language Assessment of Linguistic Minority Students."
Workshops: "Assessment Instruments for Non-English Speaking Handicapped Students" (2 hrs)
Consultancy: Psychological Assessment; Bilingual Special Education Program Development

Robert S. Rueda
Assistant Professor
Department of Special Education
Arizona State University
Tempe, AZ 85281 (602) 965-1457

Publications: "Referential Communication Skill Levels of Moderately Retarded Children" (Co-authored with K. Chan. *American Journal of Mental Deficiency,* vol. 85, no. 1, 1980, pp. 45–52); "Review of Self-control Research with Behaviorally Disordered and Mentally Retarded Children" (Co-authored with R. Rutherford and K. Howell. In *Severe Behavior Disorders of Children and Youth: CCBD Monograph, Volume III,* edited by R. Rutherford and A. Prieto. Reston, VA: Council for Children with Behavior Disorders, Summer 1980, pp. 188–197); "Teachers' Perceptions of Competencies for Teaching Bilingual/Multicultural Exceptional Children" (Co-authored with R. Rodriguez and A. Prieto. *Exceptional Children,* in press)
Lectures: "Teachers' Perceptions of Competencies for Teaching Bilingual/ Multicultural Exceptional Children"; "Interpersonal Tactics and Communicative Strategies of Anglo-American and Mexican-American Mildly Retarded Students"; "Teaching Competencies for Bilingual/Multicultural Exceptional Children"
Workshops: Same as lecture topics (variable length)

Nadeen T. Ruiz
Bilingual Special Education Consultant
Doctoral Candidate
Stanford University
School of Education
Stanford, CA 94305 (415) 493-0288

Publications: The Bilingual Special Education Dictionary: A Resource for Parents and Professionals (B.A.B.E.L., in press)
Lectures: "Language Proficiency"; "Southwest Dialects"; "First and Second Language Acquisition"; "Bilingual Special Education"
Workshops: "Language Proficiency Assessment with Hispanic Exceptional Children" (2–5 hrs)
Consultancy: Language Proficiency; Assessment with Hispanic Exceptional Children; Bilingual Special Education

Eugene Scholten, PhD
School Psychologist
Holland Michigan Public Schools
633 Apple Ave
Holland, MI 49423 (616) 396-3535

Publications: "Demographic Data on the Culturally Different Child" (Michigan State publication)
Lectures: "Cultural Differences in Assessment"
Consultancy: Assessing through Language Barriers for Specific Disabilities

Dr. Stan Seidner
Assistant Dean for Research and Development
National College of Education
2840 Sheridan Rd
Evanston, IL 60201 (312) 256-5150, ext 211

Publications: Issues of Language Assessment (1982)
Lectures: "Language Assessment"; "Program Evaluation"
Workshops: "Language Assessment" (45 mins–1½ hrs)
Consultancy: Available to colleges/universities, school systems, or government agencies

Dr. Kenneth H. Sennett
Special Education Department Head
Brockton Public Schools
43 Crescent St
Brockston, MA 02401 (617) 580-7525

Publications: The Brockton Battery: Special Needs Assessment for Bilingual Students—Tests; "Special Needs Assessments for Linguistic Minority Students" (ERIC Document)
Lectures: "Assessment for Special Needs Minority Students"
Consultancy: Assessment; Reading instruction

Benjamin Silva, Jr.
Director, Title VII
Brockton Public Schools
43 Crescent St
Brockton, MA 02401 (617) 580-7508
Lectures: "The Cape Verdean Bilingual Student Cultural Adjustments and Associated Problems"
Workshops: "Cultural Adjustment of Cape Verdean Students" (2 hrs)
Resource Materials: Videocassette on Cape Verde and its people

M. Patricia Simmons, PhD
Professor, Faculty Coordinator

CSULA-Aztec Head Start Project
California State University
5151 State University Dr
Los Angeles, CA 90032 (213) 224-3711

Publications: "Approach-Avoidance Attitude toward Handicapped"; "Differential Impact of Handicaps"; "Non-verbal Language Inventory" (scale for teacher use)
Lectures: "Working with Parents of Young Handicapped Children in a Bilingual Setting"
Workshops: "Assessing Parent Attitudes toward Programs"; "Attitudes toward Handicapped and Language Skills in Young Children"
Consultancy: Parent Training; Attitude or Assessment; Staff Evaluation
Resource Materials: Items mentioned in publications area are for sale from Dr. Simmons
Additional Comments: Seven years of experience as an administrator and have training with programs serving this Spanish-speaking population. Worked with Head Start, Infant-Family Projects, and with handicapped and nonhandicapped children and their families.

Eydie Sloane
Inservice Specialist
FDLRS-SOUTH
3196 SW 155 St
Miami, FL 33155 (305) 666-1995

Lectures: "Mainstreaming the Bilingual Handicapped Child"
Workshops: Same as lecture topic (variable length)

Ricardo Sosapavon
Specialist
Los Angeles Unified Schools
3421 West 2nd St
Los Angeles, CA 90004 (213) 625-6232

Lectures: "Identification of Severely Handicapped Students as LEP Students"; "Lau vs. Nichols and the Exceptional Child"; "Mexican American Culture and History"; "The Bilingual Learning Handicapped Student"
Workshops: Spanish reading (1½ hrs); English as a Second Language (1½ hrs); Spanish Oral Language Development (1½ hrs); Bilingual Methodology (1½ hrs); Public Law 94-142 (1½ hrs); Basic Inventory of Natural Language (BINL) Trainer (3 hrs)
Consultancy: Identification of Exceptional Children as LEP Students; Parents Rights and Responsibilities: P.L. 94-142; Bilingual Programs for Exceptional Students

Dr. John Spiridakis
Director, Bilingual Education Program

Saint. John's University
Jamaica, NY 11439 (212) 990-6161
Publications: Self Concept and Education (Athens, Greece: Alkyon Press); ''Bilingual Special Education in Greece and the US'' (ERIC Document, November 1981)
Lectures: ''Bilingual Special Education in Greece and the US''
Workshops: ''Bilingual Special Education'' (1 hr)
Consultancy: Program Evaluations of New York Schools' Bilingual Special Education Projects

Annette Tessier, EdD
Professor and Program Coordinator of Centro de Ninos y Padres Early Intervention Program
Department of Special Education
California State University
5151 State University Dr
Los Angeles, CA 90032 (213) 224-3711
Publications: ''Parents Learn to Help Themselves'' (Co-authored with S. Barton. In *Early Education in Spanish-Speaking Communities,* edited by P. L. Trohanis. New York: Walker, 1978)
Lectures: ''Working with Young Handicapped Children and Their Families in a Hispanic Community''; ''Child Abuse and the Handicapped Child''
Workshops: ''Parents Advocacy''; ''Parents as Peer Counselors''; ''Parents as Teachers of Their Young Special Child'' (variable length)
Consultancy: Development of Programs for High Risk and Young Children with Special Needs
Resource Materials: ''The Handicapped Child: Infancy through Preschool'' (Filmstrip series, Concept Media, 2493 DuBridge Ave, Irvine, CA 92714)

Barbara M. Thomson
Junior High Bilingual Teacher
Lee Mathson Community School
2050 Kammerer Ave
San Jose, CA 95116 (408) 251-3232
Publications: ''The Gifted Bilingual Student'' (ERIC Document)
Additional Comments: Area of research is ''Integrated Programs for Gifted Students'' and ''Discovering the Gifted Bilingual Student.''

Eleanor Thonis, PhD
Consultant, Bilingual Education
Marysville Joint Unified School District
1919 B St
Marysville, CA 95901 (916) 742-5501

Publications: Speech, Print and Thought in Bilingual Bicultural Education (California State Department of Education, 1980); *Reading Instruction for Language Minority Students* (California State Department of Education, 1981)

Dr. Richard L. Towers

Director of Interagency, Alternative, and Supplementary Programs
Montgomery County, Maryland Public Schools
850 Hungerford Dr
Rockville, MD 20850 (301) 279-3246

Publications: "Early Intervention Programs in Maryland County Public Schools"; "Bilingual Assessment of LEP Students"
Lectures: "Cross-Cultural Assessment"; "Administrating and Organizing Interdisciplinary Special Education Programs"
Consultancy: Organization and Management of Interdisciplinary Bilingual Special Education Programs

Maria Luisa Vallejo

Resource Specialist
New England Bilingual Education Service Center
345 Blackstone Blvd
Providence, RI 02906 (401) 272-7133

Publications: "The Bilingual Child with Special Needs: Cultural Considerations in Evaluation"; "Vocational Education for LEP Youngsters with Special Needs"
Lectures: "Assessment (in general) and Assessment (for teaching)"; "The LEP with Special Needs and His Family"
Workshops: Same as lecture topics (variable length)
Consultancy: Testing; Assessment; Adaptation of Materials; Programming
Additional Comments: The NEBESC is a national resource center. As part of a network, it has access to many resources.

Carole Veir, EdD

Assistant Professor
Department of Special Education
College of Education
Arizona State University
Tempe, AZ 85283 (602) 965-1455

Publications: "Legal Aspects of Bilingual Special Education" (in progress)
Lectures: "Teacher Competencies and Issues in Training for Bilingual Special Education"
Workshops: Educational Evaluation of Bilingual Special Education Students (3 hrs); Linking Bilingual and Special Education to Form a Successful Team (3 hrs)
Consultancy: Educational Evaluation; Testing Procedures; Successful Teaming of Bilingual and Special Education Personnel; Educational Evaluation of Indian Children; Changing Attitudes; Identification of Special Education Students (who are also bilingual/monolingual)
Resource Materials: Resource Directory: Bilingual Special Education Personnel; A Comprehensive Bibliography of Bilingual Special Education Reading
Additional Comments: Specialist in legal and policy issues related to bilingual/special education and work with adult bilingual special education students.

Dan Watson
Guidance Coordinator
San Diego County Department of Education
6401 Linda Vista Rd
San Diego, CA 92111   (714) 292-3570

Publications: Non-Discriminatory Assessment: A Practitioner's Guide; Non-Discriminatory Assessment: A Trainer's Manual
Lectures: "Cultural Awareness"; "Appropriate Test Use"; "Non-Discriminatory Assessment"; "Assessment/Identification of Bilingual Special Education Students"
Workshops: "Non-Discriminatory Assessment/Appropriate Assessment for All" (4–8 hrs)
Consultancy: Assisting/Directing/Training School Psychologists/Resource Specialists/Special Education Teachers
Resource Materials: Non-Discriminatory Assessment: A Practitioner's Guide (350 pp. $16)
Additional Comments: Extensive work with school psychologists and special educators both in training for testing and assistance with specific children and complete bilingual evaluation of children.

Rafaela E. Weffer, PhD
Director, Division of Human Development
DePaul University
802 W Belden, 3rd Fl
Chicago, IL 60614   (312) 321-8390

Publications: "Bilinguality and Its Implications in Assessment" (ERIC Document, 1980); "Factors to be Considered when Assessing Bilingual Hispanic Children" (ERIC Document, 1981)
Lectures: "Assessment"; "Parent Training"; "Interaction of Bilinguality and Learning Disabled"
Workshops: Same as lecture topics (variable length)

Dr. Florence D. Weiner
Associate Professor
Marymount Manhattan College
PO Box 714
Amherst, MA 01004   (413) 253-5336

Publications: "Spanish Picture Vocabulary Test: Adaptation and Restandardization of the P.P.V.T." (Dunn, 1965)
Lectures: "Language Assessment of Bilingual Children"; "Bilingual Interferences in the Speech and Language Assessment of Hispanic Children"
Workshops: "Contrast and Comparison of Language Development in Bilingual Populations" (3 hrs)
Consultancy: Speech and Language Testing; Programming for Bilingual Children

Lenore Higgins Worcester

Associate Research Professor
University of Maine at Orono
305 Shibles Hall
Orono, ME 04469 (207) 581-2691

Publications: "Franco American Learning Disabled College Student"; "Gifted/ Franco American" (ERIC Documents)
Lectures: "Learning Disabilities and Franco Americans" "Gifted Franco Americans"
Workshops: "How to Identify the Learning Disabled-Bilingual Child"; "Characteristics/Learning Style" (1½ hrs–all day)
Consultancy: Assisting Teachers and Parents of the Franco/LD/Gifted; Assisting School Systems in Adapting Curriculum
Additional Comments: Fifteen years of work experience with learning disabled and gifted populations; past 5 years with the Franco/American population.

Julie Tu Wu

Associate Professor
Hunter College, City University of New York
695 Park Ave
PO Box 1739
New York, NY 10021 (212) 570-5433

Publications: "Your Handicapped Child's Right to Education" (Translation, New York State Document, 1980)
Lectures: "Helping Bilingual Teachers Understand Children with Special Learning Difficulties and Behavior Disorders"
Workshops: "Training Regular Elementary School Teachers to Use a Screening Device for Identifying Special Learning Problems"
Consultancy: Identifying Children with Different Cultural and Language Backgrounds Who Need Special Education
Resource Materials: "A Screening Device for Diagnosing Basic Learning Problems" (a kit with manipulative materials)

Appendix
Producers and Distributors
of Materials

Association for Childhood
  Education International
3615 Wisconsin Ave, NW
Washington, DC 20016

Bank Street College of Education
Division of Graduate Programs
610 W 112th St
New York, NY 10025

Barnell Loft, Ltd
958 Church St
Baldwin, NY 11510

Batey Bilingual Media Inc
80 Fifth Ave, Rm 906
New York, NY 10011

Bell & Howell
Audio-Visual Products Division
7100 N McCormick Rd
Chicago, IL 60645

Bilingual & Migrant Education
Toledo Public Schools
Manhattan and Elm
Toledo, OH 43608

The Bilingual Publications Co
1966 Broadway
New York, NY 10023

California State Library
Marjorie LeDonne
PO Box 2037
Sacramento, CA 95809
[Note: Materials available on loan
  only; not for sale.]

CAR-LA Educational Enterprises
3113 Malcolm
Los Angeles, CA 90034

Children's Book and Music Center
5373 W Pico
Los Angeles, CA 90019

Churchill Films
662 N Robertson Blvd
Los Angeles, CA 90069

Coronet Multimedia Co
65 E Southwater St
Chicago, IL 60601

Crawley Educational Materials
PO Box 757
Brea, CA 92621

Cypress International
PO Box 26504
San Jose, CA 95159

Developmental Learning Materials
7440 Natchez Ave
Niles, IL 60648

Dexter and Westbrook, Ltd
958 Church St
Baldwin, NY 11510

Dissemin/Action Project
3705 S George Mason Dr
Falls Church, VA 22041

Dormac, Inc
PO Box 752
Beaverton, OR 97075

Editorial Kapelusz S.A.
Moreno 372—1091 Buenos Aires
Argentina

Educational Design, Inc
47 W 13th St
New York, NY 10011

Educational Projections Co
1911 Pickwick Ave
Glenview, IL 60025

Educational Teaching Aids
Division of A. Daigger & Co
159 W Kinzie St
Chicago, IL 60610

Encyclopedia Britannica
   Educational Corp
425 N Michigan Ave
Chicago, IL 60611

ERIC Clearinghouse on
   Handicapped and Gifted
   Children
Council for Exceptional Children
1920 Association Dr
Reston, VA 22091

European Book Co
925 Larkin St
San Francisco, CA 94109

Eye Gate Media
146-01 Archer Ave
Jamaica, NY 11435

Fearon Pitman Publishers, Inc
6 Davis Dr
Belmont, CA 94002

Flame Co
167 Kelly Blvd
Staten Island, NY 10314

Folkways Records
43 W 61st St
New York, NY 10023

Follett Publishing Co
1010 W Washington Blvd
Chicago, IL 60607

Houghton Mifflin
1 Beacon St
Boston, MA 02107

Ideal School Supply Co
11000 S Lavergre Ave
Oak Lawn, IL 60453

Innovative Sciences, Inc
300 Broad St
Stanford, CT 06901

Institute of Modern Languages
2622 Pittman Dr
Silver Spring, MD 20910

Janus Book Publishers
2501 Industrial Pkwy W
Hayward, CA 94545

King Features
235 E 45th St
New York, NY 10017

Lakeshore Curriculum Materials
2695 E Dominquez St
PO Box 6261
Carson, CA 90749

Learning Corp of America
1350 Ave of Americas
New York, NY 10019

Lowell and Lynwood, Ltd
958 Church St
Baldwin, NY 11510

Media Marketing, Inc
PO Box 7184
5307 Lee Hwy
Arlington, VA 22207

Melton Peninsula, Inc
1949 Stemmons Freeway,
   Suite 690
Dallas, TX 75207

Miller-Brody Productions, Inc
Random House
342 Madison Ave
New York, NY 10017

Modern Education Corporation
PO Box 721 •
Tulsa, OK 74101

Mosier Materials
Box 3036
San Bernardino, CA 92413

Multi Dimensional
   Communications, Inc
Orange Strawberry Filmstrips
45 Browndate Pl
Port Chester, NY 10573

National Center for the
   Development of Bilingual
   Education
3700 Ross Ave, Box 103
Dallas, TX 75204

National Clearinghouse for
   Bilingual Education (NCBE)
1300 Wilson Blvd, Suite B2-11
Rosslyn, VA 22209

National Educational Laboratory
PO Box 1003
Austin, TX 78767

National Information Center for
   Special Education Materials
   (NICSEM)
University of Southern California
University Park
Los Angeles, CA 90007

National Textbook Company
8259 Niles Center Rd
Skokie, IL 60076

Newby Visualanguage, Inc
Box 121-AV
Eagleville, PA 19408

Office of Special Education
US Department of Education
Regional Office Bldg
7th & D Sts, SW
Washington, DC 20202

Open Court Publishing Company
PO Box 599
LaSalle, IL 61301

Parents' Magazine Films
Dept 132, 52
Vanderbuilt Ave
New York, NY 10017

Prentice-Hall
Englewood Cliffs, NJ 07632

A.H. & A.W. Reed
182 Wakefield St, Wellington
29 Dacre St, Auckland
51 Whiting St, Antarmon,
New South Wales

Regents Publishing Co, Inc
2 Park Ave
New York, NY 10016

The Regents of the University
    of Colorado—Boulder
Department of Education
Boulder, CO 80309

Santillana Publishing Co
575 Lexington Ave
New York, NY 10022

Scott, Foresman & Co
1900 E Lake Ave
Glenview, IL 60025

Seaside Education Associates
Zero Elm St
Manchester, MA 01944

Social Studies School Service
10,000 Culver Blvd, Dept 40
PO Box 802
Culver City, CA 90230

South Pacific Commission
Publications Bureau
32 Bridge St, Sydney
PO Box N324 Grosvenor St
N.S.W. 2000, Australia

Teaching Resources Corp
50 Pond Park Rd
Hingham, MA 02043

Ventura Press
PO Box 1076
Guerneville, CA 95441

Voluntad Publishers, Inc
Exchange Park, Suite 220 S
7800 Shoal Creek Blvd
Austin, TX 78757

YAK Corporation
PO Box 99026
San Diego, CA 92109

Yardbird Publishing Co, Inc
PO Box 2370, Station A
Berkeley, CA 94701

Bibliography

In gathering citations for this bibliography, the following databases were searched: National Clearinghouse for Bilingual Education (NCBE Bibliographic Database); ERIC (Educational Resources Information Center); ECER (Exceptional Child Education Resources); DISS (Comprehension Dissertation Abstracts); and PSYC (Psychological Abstracts). In addition, the compilers surveyed *Educational Administration Abstracts, Education Index,* and *Language Behavior Abstracts.*

Abbott, R. E., and Peterson, P. J. "Learning Disabilities—They're All Around You." Paper presented at the International Bilingual/Bicultural Education Conference, Chicago, IL, May 1975. ERIC document ED 128 529.

Almanza, Helen P., and Mosley, William J. "Curriculum Adaptations and Modifications for Culturally Diverse Handicapped Children," *Exceptional Children* 46 (8) (May 1980): 608–14.

Ambert, Alba N., et al. *Manual for Identification of Limited-English Proficiency Students with Special Needs.* Boston, MA: Massachusetts Department of Education [Division of Special Education, Bureau of Program Development and Evaluation, 31 Saint James, 02116], 1980.

Anderson, T., and Boyer, M. *Bilingual Schooling in the United States.* Washington, DC: Superintendent of Documents, US Government Printing Office, n.d.

Archuleta, Katherine, and Cervantes, Hermes T. "Misplaced Child: Does Linguistically Different Mean Learning Disabled?" University Park Press, 1981. Baltimore, MD: Paper presented at the Bilingual Bicultural Education Conference, Seattle, WA, May 1979.

Assessment Instruments in Bilingual Education. A Descriptive Catalog of 342 Oral and Written Tests. Los Angeles, CA: National Dissemination and Assessment Center, 1980.

Association for Cross Cultural Education and Social Studies. *Issues in Bilingual/Bicultural Special Education Personnel Preparation: Workshop Report.* Washington, DC: The Association [401 M St, Suite 1006, 20024], 1980.

Ayala-Vásquez, Nancy. "Bilingual Special Education: Ahora." In *Bilingual Education,* by Hernan Lafontaine, et al, pp. 261–67. Wayne, NJ: Avery, 1978.

Baca, Leonard M. "A Survey of Testing, Labeling and Placement Procedures to Assign Mexican-American Students into Classes for Educable Mentally Retarded in the Southwest." EdD dissertation, University of Northern Colorado, 1974.

————. "What's Going on in the Bilingual Special Education Classroom," *Teaching Exceptional Children* 7 (February 1974): 25.

Baca, Leonard M., and Bransford, Jim. "Meeting the Needs of the Bilingual Handicapped Child," *Momentum* 12 (2) (May 1981): 26–29, 49–51.

Baca, Leonard M., and Lane, Karen. "A Dialogue on Cultural Implications for Learning," *Exceptional Children* 40 (May 1974): 552–63.

Bailey, Donald B., and Harbin, Gloria L. "Nondiscriminatory Evaluation," *Exceptional Children* 46 (8) (May 1980): 590–96.

Bell, Paul W. "A Beginning Reading Program for the Linguistically Handicapped." 1966. ERIC document ED 015 043.

Bergin, Victoria. *Special Education Needs in Bilingual Programs*. Rosslyn, VA: National Clearinghouse for Bilingual Education, 1980. ECER document EC 131 729.

Bilingual-Bicultural Education and English-as-a-Second Language Education: A Framework for Elementary and Secondary Schools. Sacramento, CA: California State Department of Education, 1974. ERIC document ED 121 095.

"Bilingual Early Childhood Program. Level I." Austin, TX: National Educational Laboratory, 1972.

Blatt, B. "Bandwagons Also Go to Funerals," *Journal of Learning Disabilities* 12 (4) (April 1979): 222–24.

Bransford, L. A.; Baca, Leonard; and Lane, Karen, eds. *Cultural Diversity in a Highly Exceptional Child*. Reston, VA: Council for Exceptional Children, 1974.

Brislin, Richard, et al. *Cross-Cultural Research Methods*. New York: John Wiley, 1973.

Bruck, M. "Switching Out of French Immersion," *Interchange of Educational Policy* 9 (4) (1979): 86–94.

Bruck, M., et al. "Effects of French Immersion Programs on Children with Language Disabilities: A Preliminary Report." January 1975. ERIC document ED 125 242.

Bryen, Diane N. "Special Education and the Linguistically Different Child," *Exceptional Children* 40 (8) (May 1974): 589–99.

————. "Speech-Sound Discrimination Ability on Linguistically Unbiased Tests," *Exceptional Children* 42 (4) (January 1976): 195–201.

Carrasquillo, Angela. "New Directions for Special Education through a Bilingual Bicultural Approach." Paper presented at the Annual International Convention, The Council for Exceptional Children, Atlanta, GA, April 11–15, 1977. ERIC document ED 139 173.

CARTEL: Annotations of Bilingual Multicultural Materials with Cumulative Indexes for Volume IV. Austin, TX: Dissemination and Assessment Center for Bilingual Education, 1978.

Casso, Henry J. " A Descriptive Study of Three Legal Challenges for Placing Mexican-American and Other Linguistically and Culturally Different Children into Educably Mentally Retarded Classes." EdD dissertation, University of Massachusetts, 1973.

Castaneda, Alfredo. *Introduction to Cognitive Styles*. Austin, TX: Dissemination Center for Bilingual/Bicultural Education, 1974.

Cervenka, E. J. *Project BUILD: "Bilingual Understanding Incorporates Learning Disabilities"—An ESEA Title VII Basic Bilingual Program*. New York: Community School District 4, 1979. ERIC document ED 190 692.

Chermak, G. D. "Review of Issues in Black Dialect: A Proposed Two-Way Bilingual Educational Approach and Considerations for the Congenitally Deaf Child," *Psychology in the Schools* 13 (1) (January 1976): 101–09.

Chinn, P. "The Exceptional Minority Child: Issues and Some Answers," *Exceptional Children* 45 (7) (April 1979): 532–36.

Cohen, B. H. *Evaluating Bilingual Education Programs*. Hingham, MA: Teaching Resource Corp., 1979.

Comprehensive Infant Intervention Program: End-of-Year Report: July 1, 1978–June 30, 1979. San Antonio, TX: Edgewood Independent School District, 1979.

Compton, C. *A Guide to 65 Tests for Special Education*. Belmont, CA: Fearon, 1980.

Conceptos Basicos. New York: McGraw-Hill, 1975.

Condon, Elaine C.; Peters, Janice Y.; and Sueiro-Ross, Carmen. *Special Education and the Hispanic Child: Cultural Perspectives*. Philadelphia, PA: Teacher Corps Mid-Atlantic Network, 1979.

Correia, L. M. *Escala de Comportamentos Para Criancas (Behavior Measures for Children)*. Providence, RI: National Portuguese Materials Development Center, 1980.

Cortes, Lydia. "A Student's Reaction to Bilingual Special Education." Paper presented at the Annual International Convention, Council for Exceptional Children, Atlanta, GA, April 11–15, 1977. ERIC document ED 139 174.

Culture-free Tests. Princeton, NJ: Educational Service/ERIC Clearinghouse on Tests, Measurements, and Evaluation, 1980.

Cummins, James. "Bilingualism and the Development of Metalinguistic Awareness," *Journal of Cross-Cultural Psychology* 9 (2) (1978): 131–49.

Cunha, P. "Bridging the Gap," *Bilingual Journal* 2 (3) (Spring 1978): 18–20.

DeAvila, Edward, and Havassy, Barbara. *I.Q. Tests and Minority Children*. Stockton, CA: Multilingual Assessment Program, 1974.

Decano, Pio. "Asian and Pacific-American Exceptional Children: A Conversation," *Teacher Education and Special Education* 2 (4) (Summer 1979): 33–36.

Deignan, Margaret C., and Ryan, Kathleen E. *Annotated Bibliography of Bilingual Teaching Materials Applicable to the Special Learning Needs of Spanish-Dominant Special Education Pupils*. 1979. ERIC document ED 196 178.

Diggs, Ruth W. "Education Across Cultures," *Exceptional Children* 40 (May 1974): 578–83.

Downing, J. "Results of Teaching Reading in I.T.A. to Children with Cognitive Defects," *Reading World* 18 (3) (March 1979): 290–99.

Dye, Joan, and Frankfort, Nancy. "Suggestions for Expanding Teaching Ideas to Prepare for Mainstreaming Disabled ESL Learners," *Education Unlimited* 3 (1) (January/February 1981): 33–36.

Eaton, Phoebe A. "A Comparison of WISC IQ Subtests, and Factor Scores of Spanish-Surnamed Children Identified as Mentally Retarded." EdD dissertation, University of Northern Colorado, 1972.

Ehrlich, Alen, et al. "Tests in Spanish and Other Languages, English as a Second Language and Non-verbal Tests for Bilingual Programs: An Annotated B.E.A.U.R.A. Bibliography," New York: Project Best, Hunter College Division [560 Lexington Ave, 10022], 1974.

"Evaluation Instruments for Bilingual Education: An Annotated Bibliography." Austin, TX: Dissemination Center for Bilingual/Bicultural Education [7703 N Lamar Blvd, 78752], n.d.

Evans, J. *Identification and Supplementary Instruction for Handicapped Children in a Regular Bilingual Program*. Austin, TX: Southwest Educational Development Laboratory, 1976. ERIC document ED 123 891.

———. *A Project to Develop Curriculum for Four-Year-Old Handicapped Mexican American Children. Final Report. Appendix*. 2 vols. Austin, TX: Southwest Educational Development Laboratory, 1974. ERIC documents ED 121 046 and ED 121 047.

———. "Survey of Tests Administered to Preschool Children in Texas." Austin, TX: Southwest Educational Development Laboratory, 1975. ERIC document ED 122 945.

————. *Working with Parents of Handicapped Children*. Reston, VA: Council for Exceptional Children, 1976.

"Exceptional Children Conference Papers: Early Childhood Education." Five conference papers presented at the Annual International Convention, The Council for Exceptional Children, Dallas, TX, April 22–27, 1973. ERIC document ED 078 631.

Gallegos, Robert L., et al. "Bilingual/Bicultural Education—Special Education: An Interface." Paper presented at the Annual International Convention, Council for Exceptional Children, April 1980, Philadelphia, PA.

Garza, S. G. *Language Assessment Identifying LESA's*. 1976. ERIC document ED 144 415.

Gavillan-Torres, Eva M. "An Interdisciplinary Approach to the Education of Hispanic Handicapped Children," *Education Unlimited* 2 (4) (September-October 1980): 24–26.

Gimon, Alexander T. "Maternal Expectancies: Effects of Their Modification on Training Behavior of Puerto Rican Mothers toward Their Retarded Children." PhD dissertation, Yeshiva University, 1973.

Gonzalez, Edna T. "A Comparison of the Level of Aspiration between Hispanic Children in Bilingual and Regular Special Education Programs." PhD dissertation, University of Connecticut, 1980.

Gonzales, Eloy, and Ortiz, Leroy. "Social Policy and Education Related to Linguistically and Culturally Different Groups," *Journal of Learning Disabilities* 10 (6) (June/July 1977): 11–17.

Gonzalez, Gustavo. "Language, Culture, and Exceptional Children," *Exceptional Children* 40 (8) (May 1974): 565–70.

Goodale, Ronda, and Soden, Marcia. "Disproportionate Placement of Black and Hispanic Students in Special Education Programs." Paper presented at the Council for Exceptional Children Conference on The Exceptional Bilingual Child. New Orleans, LA, February 1981. ECER document EC 133 340.

Grant, June M. "A Study of the Development of Eight Hearing-Impaired Preschool Children from Spanish-Speaking Homes." PhD dissertation, The University of Texas—Austin, 1975.

Guide to Resources for Bilingual/Bicultural Education. Hightstown, NJ: Northeast ALRC/RRC Region 9, 1975.

Hagen, John W.; and Hallahan, Daniel P. "A Language Training Program for Preschool Migrant Children," *Exceptional Children* 37 (April 1971): 606–07.

Hall, J. W. "Testing of Non-English Speaking Patients," *Audiology and Hearing Education* 2 (4) (June/July 1976): 11, 14–16, 19, 30.

Harber, Jean. "The Bilingual Child with Learning Problems." 1976. ERIC document ED 143 149.

Hatfield, Nancy, et al. "Deaf Students' Language Competency: A Bilingual Perspective," *American Annals of the Deaf* 123 (7) (November 1978): 847–51.

Hausman, Ralph M. "Efficacy of Three Learning Potential Assessment Procedures with Mexican American Educable Mentally Retarded Children." PhD dissertation, George Peabody College for Teachers, 1972.

Hickey, T. "Bilingualism and the Assessment of Intelligence and Verbal Learning Ability," *Exceptional Children* 39 (1) (1972): 24–28.

Hill, Willie Kiah. "Variations in the Rationale of Referrals Leading to Educable Mentally Retarded Placement of Anglo, Black and Spanish-Speaking Students." EdD dissertation, Rutgers University, 1975.

Hilliard, Asa G. "Cultural Diversity and Special Education," *Exceptional Children* 46 (8) (May 1980): 584–88.

Hoernicke, Placido A. "The Morphological Development of Language in School Age Chicano Educable Mentally Retarded." EdD dissertation, University of Northern Colorado, 1974.

Instructional Materials: Selection and Purchase. Revised Edition. New York: Association of American Publishers, 1976. ERIC document ED 130 380.

Instructional Materials Selection Guide. Bilingual/Bicultural ESL. Los Angeles, CA: California State University, National Dissemination and Assessment Center, 1978. ERIC document ED 168 295.

"Issues in Bilingual/Bicultural Special Education Personnel Preparation." Proceedings from February 4-5, 1980 Conference sponsored by the Association for Cross Cultural Education and Social Studies, 401 M St, Suite 1006, Washington, DC 20024.

Jaramillo, Mari-luci. "Cultural Conflict Curriculum and the Exceptional Child," *Exceptional Children* 40 (May 1974): 585–87.

Jensen, A. R. "Do Schools Cheat Minority Children?" *Educational Research* 14 (November 1971): 3–28.

Jones, Reginald L., ed. *Mainstreaming and the Minority Child.* Reston, VA: Council for Exceptional Children, 1976.

Jorstad, Dorothy. "Psycho-linguistic Learning Disabilities in 20 Mexican-American Students," *Journal of Learning Disabilities* 4 (March 1971): 26.

Juaŕez, Manuela. "Special Education in the Bilingual Program." Paper presented at the 3rd National Conference on Multicultural Curriculum and Materials, San Francisco, CA, 1976. [Copies available from Manuela Juarez, Miller Speech and Hearing Clinic, Texas Christian University, Fort Worth, TX 76129.]

Kamp, Susan H., and Chinn, Philip C. *A Multiethnic Curriculum for Special Education Students*. Reston, VA: Council for Exceptional Children, 1982.

Killian L. R. "WISC, Illinois Test of Psycholinguistic Abilities, and Bender Visual-Motor Gestalt Test Performance of Spanish-American Kindergarten and First-Grade School Children," *Journal of Consulting and Clinical Psychology* 37 (1) (August 1971): 38–43.

Kline, Carl L., and Lee, Norma. "A Transcultural Study of Dyslexia: Analysis of Language Disabilities in 277 Chinese Children Simultaneously Learning to Read and Write in English and in Chinese," *Journal of Special Education* 6 (1) (Spring 1972): 9–26.

Landurand, Patricia, et al. *Bridging the Gap between Bilingual and Special Education*. Reston, VA: ERIC Clearinghouse on Handicapped and Gifted Children/Council for Exceptional Children, 1980.

Leonard, Carol J. "The Bilingual-Bicultural Frame of Reference from the Social Worker's Point of View." Paper presented at the World Congress on Future Special Education, Stirling, Scotland, June 1978. ERIC document ED 158 535; ECER document EC 111 936.

Lerman, A., et al. *Discovering and Meeting the Needs of Hispanic Hearing Impaired Children*. Albany, NY: New York State Education Department, Bureau of Physically Handicapped Children, 1978. ERIC document ED 155 292.

Lesser, Saal D. *Improving Bilingual Instruction and Services in Special Schools*. Brooklyn, NY: New York City Board of Education, Office of Educational Evaluation, 1975. ERIC doument ED 139 893.

Lewis, Sheri, and Reinach, Jacquelyn. "The Bi-Lingual Early Learning Filmstrip Library." New York: Miller Brody, 1970.

Lijtmaer, Ruth M. "Bilingualism and Learning Disabilities in Spanish-Speaking Children." PhD dissertation, New York University, 1978.

Locks, N. A.; Pletcher, B. A.; and Reynolds, D. F. *Language Assessment Instruments for Limited-English-Speaking Students. A Needs Analysis*. Washington, DC: National Institute of Education (DHEW), 1978.

Luetke, B. "Questionnaire Results from Mexican-American Parents of Hearing Impaired Children in the United States," *American Annals of the Deaf* 21 (6) (December 1976): 565-68.

McAreavey, James Patrick. "An Analysis of Selected Educationally Handicapped South Dakota Sioux Indian Children's Responses to the Weschsler Intelligence Scale for Children and Wide Range Achievement Test of Reading." EdD dissertation, University of Colorado, 1975.

———. "An Analysis of Selected Educationally Handicapped South Dakota Sioux Indian Children's Responses to the Weschsler Intelligence Scale for Children and Wide Range Achievement Test of Reading." EdD dissertation, University of Colorado, 1975.

McCabe, R. *McCabe's Test Handbook: A Guide to Tests Used by Speech Pathologists, Learning Disabilities Specialists and Special Educators.* Tigard, OR: C. C. Publications, 1978.

McConnell, Beverly B. "IBI (Individualized Bilingual Instruction): A Validated Program Model Effective with Bilingual Handicapped Children." Paper presented at the Council for Exceptional Children Conference on The Exceptional Bilingual Child, New Orleans, LA, February 1981. ERIC document ED 203 648; ECER document EC 133 333.

McCormick, David P. " 'Occult' Bilingualism in Children with School Problems," *Journal of School Health* 50 (2) (February 1980): 84–87.

McGrath, G. D., et al. "Investigation of Mental Retardation in Relation to Bilingual and Subcultural Factors." 1960. ERIC document ED 002 810.

McLure, William P., et al. "Bilingualism and Special Education." In "Special Education: Needs—Costs—Methods of Financing. A Report of a Study." Springfield, IL: Illinois State School Problems Commission, 1975. ERIC document ED 106 985.

McShane, D., and Mitchell, J. "Middle Ear Disease, Hearing Loss and Educational Problems of American Indian Children," *Journal of American Indian Education* 19 (1) (October 1979): 7–11.

MacGregor, M. "Handle with Care: Assessing Diverse Children," *American Journal of Orthopsychiatry* 45 (2) (March 1975): 208–09.

Madachy, J. L., et al. "The Role of CAI and Video Tapes as Instructional Supplements to an English Language Program for the Hearing Impaired." Paper presented at the Annual Meeting of the Association for the Development of Computer Based Instructional Systems, Dallas, TX, 1978. ERIC document ED 160 085.

Madigan, Gerald. "El Mundo del Trabajo." St. Paul, MN: EMC, 1975.

Mangum, Melvin E., Jr. "Familial Identification in Black, Anglo and Chicano Mentally Retarded Children Using Kinetic Family Drawing." EdD dissertation, University of Northern Colorado, 1975.

Marion, Robert. "Minority Parent Involvement in the IEP Process: A Systematic Model Approach," *Focus on Exceptional Children* 10 (8) (January 1979): 1–14.

Martinez, Herminio. *Special Education and the Hispanic Child.* ERIC Clearinghouse on Urban Education, 1981. [UDS #74]

Massachusetts Advocacy Center. *Double Jeopardy.* Boston, MA: The Center [2 Park Square, 02116], n.d.

Massachusetts Department of Education. "Diagnosis and Intervention in Bilingual Special Education: Searching for New Alternatives (Proceedings)." Boston, MA: The Department, Division of Special Education, Bureau of Program Development and Evaluation [31 Saint James, 02116], May 1980.

Mercer, J. "I.Q. The Lethal Label," *Psychology Today* 6 (1972): 44–47.

Miller, Niklas. "The Bilingual Child in the Speech Therapy Clinic," *British Journal of Disorders of Communication* 13 (1) (1978): 17–30.

Milne, Nidia Moreno. "Learning Centers for the Bilingual Bicultural Handicapped Child." Paper presented at the Annual International Convention of the Council for Exceptional Children, May 2–5, 1978, Kansas City, MO. 8p. ERIC document ED 153 434.

Moustafa, M. "Picture Books for Oral Language for Non-English Speaking Children: A Bibliography," *Reading Teacher* 33 (8) (May 1980): 914–19.

Mowder, B. A. "Assessing the Bilingual Handicapped Student," *Psychology in the Schools* 16 (1) (January 1979): 42–50.

———."A Strategy for the Assessment of Bilingual Handicapped Children." *Psychology in the Schools* 17 (1) (January 1980): 7–11.

Muller, M. C. *Itinerant Bilingual Services Program for Title I Eligible CRMD Children: January-June 1975*. Brooklyn, NY: New York City Board of Education, Office of Educational Evaluation, 1975. ERIC document ED 138 698.

Murphy, Elizabeth A. "The Classroom: Meeting the Needs of the Culturally Different Child—The Navajo Nation," *Exceptional Children* 40 (May 1974): 601–08.

Newman, Lawrence. "Bilingual Education," *Deaf American* 25 (9) (May 1973): 12–13.

Nickoloff, Elia George. "The Hearing Impaired American Indian in the Vocational Rehabilitation Process." EdD dissertation, The University of Arizona, 1975.

Nondiscriminatory Testing: A Selective Bibliography. Reston, VA: Council for Exceptional Children, 1976. ECER document EC 091 211.

Odden, Allan, and McGuire, C. Kent. *Financing Educational Services for Special Populations: The State and Federal Roles. Working Papers in Education*. Denver, CO: Education Commission of the States, 1980. ERIC document ED 189 719.

Pages, Myrtha. "Bilingual-Bicultural Special Education in the Navajo Reservation—Myth or Reality." Paper presented at the World Congress on Future Special Education, June 25–July 1, 1978, Stirling, Scotland. ERIC document ED 158 511; ECER document EC 111 912.

Park, T.Z., et al. "Issues in Bilingual/Bicultural Special Education Personnel Preparation: Workshop Report" May 1980. ERIC document ED 189 795.

Perez, Fred M. ''Performance of Bilingual Children on the Spanish Version of the ITPA,'' *Exceptional Children* 46, (7) (1980): 536–41.

Peters, J. Y. *Neurologically and Perceptually Impaired Bilingual Students: Their Identification and Evaluation.* Ann Arbor, MI: University Microfilms International, 1979. [Catalog #8000874].

Peterson, P.J. ''Methods and Materials for Bilingual/Multicultural Education in the Special Education Classroom,'' *Illinois CEC Quarterly* 28 (1979): 5–10.

Pickering, M. ''Bilingual/Bicultural Education and the Speech Pathologist,'' *ASHA* 18 (5) (May 1976): 275–79.

Plata, Maximo. ''Preparing Teachers for the Mexican-American Handicapped: The Challenge and the Charge,'' *Teacher Education and Special Education* 2 (4) (Summer 1979): 21–26.

Plata, Maximo, and Jones, Pricilla. ''Bilingual Vocational Education for Handicapped Students,'' *Exceptional Children* 48 (6) (April 1982): 538–40.

Plata, Maximo, and Santos, S. L. ''Bilingual Special Education: A Challenge for the 1980's,'' *Catalyst for Change* 9 (3) (Spring 1980): 18–21.

———. ''Bilingual Special Education: A Challenge for the Future'' *Teaching Exceptional Children* 14 (3) (December 1981): 97–100.

Pletcher, B. A., et al. *A Guide to Assessment Instruments: For Limited English Speaking Students.* Palo Alto, CA: American Institutes for Research, 1978.

Pynn, M. E., et al. *Issues in Bilingual/Bicultural Special Education Personnel Preparation: Workshop Report.* Washington, DC: Association for Cross Cultural Education and Social Studies, 1980. ECER document EC 124 526.

Racial Attitude Tests. Princeton, NJ: Educational Testing Service/ERIC Clearinghouse on Tests, Measurement, and Evaluation, 1980.

Ramírez, Bruce A., and Tippeconnic, John W., III. ''Preparing Teachers of American Indian Handicapped Children,'' *Teacher Education and Special Education* 2 (4) (Summer 1979): 27–33.

Rodriguez, R. C., et al. ''Bilingualism and Biculturalism for the Special Education Classroom,'' *Teacher Education and Special Education* 2 (4) (Summer 1979): 69–74.

Rosen, Pamela, et al. ''Tests for Spanish-Speaking Children: An Annotated Bibliography.'' Princeton, NJ: Headstart Test Collection, Educational Testing Service, 1971.

Rueda, Robert S.; Rodriguez, Richard F.; and Prieto, Alfonso, G. ''Teachers' Perceptions of Competencies for Instructing Bilingual/Multicultural Exceptional Children,'' *Exceptional Children* 48 (3) (November 1981): 268–70.

Sabatino, D. A.; Hayden, D. L.; and Kelling, K. "Perceptual Language and Academic Achievement of English, Spanish and Navajo Speaking Children Referred for Special Classes," *Journal of School Psychology* 10 (1972): 39–45.

Sabatino, D. A., et al. "Special Education and the Culturally Different Child," *Exceptional Children* 39 (April 1973): 563–67.

Samude, Ronald. *Psychological Testing of American Minorities*. New York: Dodd Mead, 1975.

Santana, Jose. "Developing Educational Services for Visually Impaired Children and Youth in Puerto Rico." EdD dissertation, Columbia University, 1974.

Santiago, Ramon L. "Status of Education for Hispanics," *Educational Leadership* 38 (4) (January 1981): 292–94.

Sanua, V. D. *Bilingual Program for Physically Handicapped Children— School Year: 1974-1975*. Brooklyn, NY: New York City Board of Education, Office of Educational Evaluation, 1975. ERIC document ED 137 488.

Serfozo, Mary, et al. "I Want to Know/Quiero Saber Bilingual Learning Program." Freeport, NY: Educational Activities, 1973.

Shutt, Darold L., and Hannon, Thomas. "The Psychological Evaluation of Bi-Lingual Pupils Utilizing the Hiskey-Nebraska Test of Learning Aptitudes. A Validation Study." April 1973. ERIC document ED 109 215.

Silliman, Ben, and Alexander, David. "Legal and Ethical Considerations of School Placement for Exceptional Children." Paper presented at the Annual Career, Counseling and Vocational Education Conference on Placement, Blacksburg, VA, February 7, 1976. ECER document EC 091 006.

Silverman, R. J., et al. *Oral Language Tests for Bilingual Students: An Evaluation of Language Dominance and Proficiency Instruments*. Portland, OR: Northwest Regional Educational Laboratory, 1976.

Sirota, N. *Bilingual Program for Children in Bureau CRMD Classes- School Year: 1975-1976*. Brooklyn, NY: New York City Board of Education, Office of Educational Evaluation, 1976. ERIC document ED 137 449.

Smith, J. C. "When is a Disadvantaged a Handicap," *Journal of American Indian Education* 19 (2) (January 1980): 13–18.

Society for the Psychological Study of Social Issues. "Guidelines for Testing Minority Group Children," *Journal of Social Issues* 20 (2) (1964): 127–45.

Soeffing, Marylane Y. "New Assessment Techniques for Mentally Retarded and Culturally Different Children: A Conversation with Jane R.

Mercer," *Education and Training of the Mentally Retarded* 10 (2) (April 1975): 110–16. ECER document EC 080 989.

Special Education Index to Learner Materials. Los Angeles, CA: National Information Center for Educational Media, 1979.

Stokoe, W. C. "The Study and Use of Sign Language," *Sign Language Studies* 10 (Spring 1976): 1–36.

Testing American Indian Students. Princeton, NJ: Educational Testing Service/ERIC Clearinghouse on Tests, Measurements, and Evaluation, 1979.

Testing Bilingual Students. Princeton, NJ: Educational Testing Service/ERIC Clearinghouse on Tests, Measurement, and Evaluation, 1979.

Testing Spanish Speaking Students. Princeton, NJ: Educational Testing Service/ERIC Clearinghouse on Tests, Measurement, and Evaluation, 1979.

Topacio, C. "Special Community Needs in Bilingual Education," *Bilingual Journal* 3 (4) (Summer 1979): 17–19.

Torrance, E. P. *Discovery and Nurturance of Giftedness in the Culturally Different*. Reston, VA: Council for Exceptional Children, 1977.

Trohanis, P. L. *Early Education in Spanish-Speaking Communities*. NY: Walker, 1978.

Wagner, R. F. "Bilingualism, Multiple Dyslexia, and Polyglot Aphasia," *Academic Therapy* 12 (1) (Fall 1976): 91–97.

Watson, Bill and Van Etten, Carlene. "Bilingualism and Special Education" *Journal of Learning Disabilities* 10 (6) (June/July 1977): 331–38.

Williams, Jane C. "Improving Educational Opportunities for Mexican-American Handicapped Children." Washington, DC: Office of Education, 1968. ERIC document ED 018 326.

Williams, Judy. "Bilingual Experiences of a Deaf Child," 1968. ERIC document ED 030 092.

Wyszewianski, L. N. *Determining a Language Disorder in a Bilingual Spanish-English Population*. Ann Arbor, MI: University Microfilm International, 1977. ECER document EC 111 604. [Catalog #7732790]

Index

Compiled by Fred Ramey